TEACHER'S RESOURCE MANUAL

To Accompany

Psychology and You

by
FRANK B. MCMAHON
SOUTHERN ILLINOIS UNIVERSITY
Edwardsville

JUDITH W. MCMAHON
LINDENWOOD COLLEGE

TONY ROMANO
WILLIAM FREMD HIGH SCHOOL

Prepared by
Tony Romano

Table Of Contents

Table Of Contents

Preface

The main purpose of this manual is to provide *Practical* ways to incorporate PSYCHOLOGY AND YOU into the classroom. In fact, just flip through the manual and you'll notice that the bulk of it consists of duplication masters for students, in-class activities, lesson suggestions, and answers to textbook questions. We trust that this material will be useful to both the first-year and the experienced teacher.

Nearly all of the activities and questions listed here and in the text have been classroom tested. We believe that they are fresh and lively and that they will inspire in students an authentic appreciation of psychology. However, the teacher still needs to present these activities in a refreshing way. For example, if you assign the end-of-chapter material, collect it, write "good" at the bottom of each paper, hand it back, and do the same for each chapter, this will soon become mere routine, regardless of the quality of the textbook material. Instead, why not have something like an "Assignment Day"? On this day, students must hand in their work, but they also get a chance to share with the class what they learned. For example, students can sit in a circle and, one by one, report something interesting that they learned while completing the assignment. If you create the proper atmosphere, this kind of sharing, corny as it may seem, becomes worthwhile. If one or two students become defensive about sharing their work, simply give them the option of passing. Or here's another option. After grading students' papers, *you* can highlight various points that you found interesting and share these points with the class. In this case, you don't even need to identify which student wrote what. Or you can encourage students to display their work in class. Or give students the option of choosing which questions they will answer. For example, they can complete any five discussion questions plus any two activities. This element of control should be appealing to students. Or, while grading their work, pose questions, crack jokes, report reactions, draw pictures, and so on. In other words, all these options help demonstrate to students that their work is important—which should affect the quality of this work.

The quality of their work will also be affected, of course, by how much each assignment grade affects their quarter grades. In other words, if assignments constitute only two percent of their overall grades, don't expect much in terms of quality. Finally, the quality of their work, and the quality of their appreciation of psychology for that matter, at least for now, will depend, in large part, on *you*. We hope this creates excitement, rather than terror or dread. If it does create *some* dread, relax. If you simply communicate to students *your* excitement and enthusiasm for psychology, then they will be excited and enthused, too. If *you* are convinced that Introductory Psychology *can be* the most unique class that students ever take, then the chances are great that it will be. We hope that this manual helps in that respect.

1 The Field Of Psychology

A. CHAPTER OUTLINE

■ DEFINITION OF PSYCHOLOGY

■ RESEARCH vs. APPLIED PSYCHOLOGISTS

■ HISTORY AND ORIGIN OF PSYCHOLOGY
 Philosophy and the Greeks
  Socrates
  Plato
  Aristotle
 Astrology
 Dark and Middle Ages
 Renaissance
 Modern Times
  Charles Darwin
  Wilhelm Wundt and Introspection

■ PRESENT DAY PSYCHOLOGY
 Neurobiological Approach
 Behavioral Approach
 Humanistic Approach
 Psychoanalytic Approach
 Cognitive Approach

■ HOW TO STUDY
 SQ3R

■ OCCUPATIONAL POSSIBILITIES

B) TEXTBOOK DISCUSSION QUESTIONS

1. *How could both a research and an applied psychologist possibly be involved, let's say, in reducing someone's fear of heights?*

   A research psychologist might conduct surveys, compile statistics, gather physiological data on what occurs when fear is induced.

   An applied psychologist might take the above information and use it to help counsel or treat a phobic. Perhaps the physiological data might inspire the use of a biofeedback tool.

2. *In what ways is psychology similar to philosophy? In what ways is it different? Explain.*

   Psychology and philosophy are similar in that they both use reason, they both want to understand behavior, they both try to predict behavior to some extent, they both ask questions.

   The main difference between the two is that philosophy does not rely on the scientific method as psychology does.

3. *In your opinion, does it seem that your school promotes "Dark Ages" mentality or "Renaissance" mentality? Provide numerous examples to support your answer. Do not include any names.*

   Answers will vary. This might be a good one to discuss in class.

4. *If you were severely depressed for several weeks, would you rather have someone explain your depression to you using the neurobiological approach or the cognitive approach? Why? Explain.*

   Answers will vary. A neurobiological explanation tends to shift responsibility from the depressed person to some vague physiological area. The depressed person, in this case. is more likely to say. "Well, I can't help being depressed. It's just the way my body reacts." A cognitive explanation, on the other hand, tends to increase the depressed person's responsibility: "I'm depressed because of MY thoughts. And I CAN change my thoughts."

5. *Of the five main approaches to studying and understanding behavior (neurobiological, behaviorial, and so on), with which do you tend to agree the most and why? With which do you agree the least? Explain.*

   Answers will vary.

6. *Maria wants to ask for a raise, but begins to sweat uncontrollably every time she even gets near her boss. Using the five approaches discussed in this chapter, briefly describe how each might explain this simple behavior.*

Since these five approaches are so important, and since they will be discussed again later in the text, a detailed answer of the question appears in the Duplication section. See **MASTER 1-2**. It might be a good idea to photocopy this Master so your students have it for future reference. If you decide NOT to photocopy it perhaps you can simply make a transparency of it and discuss the answer in class.

7. *You have just read about the SQ3R method of studying, and you probably have some reactions to it. Why will you or why will you not begin to use it? Be specific — and honest.*

Answers will vary.

C) TEXTBOOK ACTIVITIES

1. This is a good initial activity to force students to skim through the textbook. You might want to do this activity as a class, where each student, after skimming through the text, writes ten or fifteen questions. Each student can then read aloud his or her five best questions. You can have a posterboard ready and jot down some of the better questions overall.

   If you like to assign independent research projects these questions could later serve as a list of possible topics.

2. Since this is the first research activity in the text. you will probably want to spell out your own requirements, especially in regards to length. It's not that length should be your foremost concern, but you need to make your expectations clear in order to receive work that meets your standards.

3. To prepare students for this activity, you could analyze your own classroom.
   Possibilities:
   a) The clock is usually placed in the back of the room so students aren't constantly watching it:
   b) The desks are too uncomfortable to sleep in: they're designed so that students face forward and sit straight (slouch and show them how you slip off):
   c) The walls are painted in bright colors to keep students awake, but they're not so bright as to distract students.

   You can go on and on.

   Once you exhaust your analysis of the classroom, you could analyze other rooms from memory: courtrooms: a living room: a room in which you might be interviewed.

4. Here are some behaviors that you might note. Females leave their homes with soft shoes and carry a set of hard shoes in their hands. When they get to work, they replace the soft shoes with the hard ones. Conclusion: Females want to be as uncomfortable as possible when they work. Males also want to be uncomfortable at work. They wear long pieces of cloth around their necks and when they arrive at work, they tighten these pieces of cloth as if they were nooses.

   This will be a good opportunity to point out the limitations of using only observations to collect data.

5. This is an activity that you may want the whole class to complete at one point or another.

6. Since this is the first activity that suggests conducting an interview, you might want to bring in a phone book or a list of mental health agencies in your area to show them how to go about finding a speaker. Emphasize that they may need to make several calls, but that persistency will pay off.

D) IN-CLASS ACTIVITIES / LESSON SUGGESTIONS

1. No matter how long you've been teaching, you probably still experience butterflies on the first day of class. Here's an activity that could help alleviate these jitters and that will help break the ice. Also, it will serve to communicate to your students that Psychology will be different than any course they've ever taken.

    As soon as the tardy bell rings, pass out an index card to each student. As you pass them out, shake each student's hand and introduce yourself. Prompt them to also introduce themselves. They will stare and giggle, of course, but you've gotten their attention. (We can introduce ourselves by shaking hands in almost any other situation, and no one will raise an eyebrow. Do it in school and you're crazy—which is something you might want to mention when you get to the chapter on abnormal behavior.)

    Slowly read aloud the following statement and have them write it down on their index cards: "This card proves beyond a shadow of a doubt that (have them insert their names) is definitely cool."

    Walk around and initialize each card and announce that these are their official cool cards. Go through a series of examples of what it means to be cool. The more personal the examples, the more effective they will be. Ideas: "I tried smoking cigarettes when I was thirteen. I hated the taste, but I liked all the things I could do with the cigarette: (demonstrate with a piece of chalk) hold it like a movie star; flick off the ashes; snap it to the ground and smash it with my foot. All those things were cool."

    Follow up the examples with the idea that we all have a desire to be cool, to be accepted by others. There's nothing wrong with this. Because of this desire, however, we sometimes go out of our way to ACT cool, instead of just being ourselves. Since they now have their official cool cards, they don't have to PROVE that they're cool. In fact, the sooner they can be themselves in class, the better the chance that they will enjoy the class and get something out of it.

    These cards, of course, will not work miracles. You will still get students who refuse to participate in your "childish" in-class activities from fear of appearing "uncool," but referring back to these cards at a later date may prompt one or two of these students to join in.

2. Prepare and hand out on the first or second day of class a syllabus that outlines your grading scale and your specific expectations. As most of you have already discovered, this is essential.

3. This is an activity for the end of the first week. Have each student pair up with someone whom they do not know. Allow them about ten minutes to interview each other. After ten minutes, have all of them sit in a circle, wherein each person will introduce his or her partner. Even the most withdrawn students handle this activity well.

    Be prepared to allow an entire class period for this activity. Some of you may be reluctant to devote this much time to an activity that doesn't really teach anything, but if conducted properly—where students LISTEN to each other—this kind of activity tends to promote an atmosphere conducive to sharing and discussing ideas.

4. Pass out Duplication **MASTER 1-1** If you flip through the Duplication / Transparency section, you'll notice that we've included a detailed Learning Goals sheet for each chapter. Note that the goals are presented in question form, making use of part two of the SQ3R method. These Learning Goals can be used as study guides for tests or as worksheets. If used as worksheets, of course, students will need to use their own papers to answer the questions since there's little free space on the Master.

5. Spend a few minutes brainstorming with your class the definition of psychology. Most classes will guess that psychology is the study of the mind. This isn't entirely incorrect, but point out that the term "mind" is vague. Instead, psychology studies behavior and then makes inferences about what goes on inside. Also, most classes will leave out the idea that psychology is scientific. Emphasize that psychology vigorously attempts to be scientific, which explains why psychology studies behavior, something that can be seen and measured and altered to some extent.

6. The distinction between an applied and a research psychologist is not a difficult one to grasp, but you will want to provide numerous examples of each since it is a distinction you will mention again and again throughout the course, especially when students ask, "So what's the point of that research?" You will smile and say, "Not all research is immediately practical." Your brilliant students will then refer back to this distinction.

   A good idea might be to bring in several copies of PSYCHOLOGY TODAY and review some of the research described in these issues. As you describe the research, have your students write down whether it primarily involves a research or an applied psychologist. This exercise will also familiarize them with the magazine.

7. Photocopy Duplication **MASTER 1-3** Students can use it as a quick reference or jot notes onto it.

8. Before you emphasize the distinction between psychology and astrology, pass out an index card to each student. Have each student write on it, "I like to write," followed by their signatures. The next day, hand them back their cards, along with another card on which you've analyzed their personalities. You can easily write a single-sentence analysis for each card by copying a line from a newspaper's daily horoscope section.

   Gauge their reactions. Do they believe that their analyses are accurate? Are the analyses scientific? Once you tactfully let them down, telling them that no analyses were actually performed, perhaps you can discuss why some of them were eager to believe the analyses. You might point out that this same eagerness may explain the popularity of astrology, despite the fact that it is obviously unscientific.

   Some of them may inquire about the validity of handwriting analysis or graphology. Graphology is NOT astrology and HAS earned the respect of many psychologists. However, even a trained graphologist would want to see more than a single sentence before rendering an analysis. Tell them that they are more complex than that, that their personalities can't be summarized through a single sentence. (Most students are fascinated by graphology. Perhaps you can invite a graphologist to visit your classes.)

9. One way to show the limitations of introspection is to bring in a poster, a piece of classical music, and a shoe (maybe just take off yours), and have students write down the sensations they experience toward each item. Write some of their reactions on the board, trying to find common reactions to the three stimuli. Are these common reactions large enough in scope to represent every person's feelings? (Before conducting this exercise, you may want to pick an object in the room and report some of your own sensations. This way, they'll have some idea of what they should write down.)

10. The chapter is very detailed in its analysis of the five approaches to studying human nature. After students read the chapter, they should be able to handle a role-playing exercise based on these approaches. Choose five volunteers to sit at the front of the classroom, each of them representing one of the five approaches. Read the following description to them and have them argue about how the situation SHOULD be interpreted or analyzed (similar to what is done in the chapter). As they argue, jot down good or accurate lines and afterwards point out these lines. Also, point out lines that weren't quite as accurate.

    "Mr. H.. has been teaching English for seven years. When he started, he would assign homework every night and return it the next day. After a few years, the quality of the work began to deteriorate and he began to doubt his ability to motivate students. As a result, it took him longer and longer to return assignments. By his sixth year, he pretty much stopped assigning homework altogether. This led to an even greater sense of failure. Now in his seventh year, he wonders what he should do with his life if he resigns from teaching."

2 Methods of Psychology

A. CHAPTER OUTLINE

■ SCIENTIFIC METHOD
  Hypothesis
  Subjects
  Variables
  Dependent Variable
  Independent Variable
  Experimental Group
  Control Group

■ OTHER METHODS FOR STUDYING BEHAVIOR
  Survey Method
  Naturalistic Observation
  Interviews
  Case-Study Method
  Psychological Tests
  Longitudinal and Cross Sectional Studies

■ Ethics of Experimentation
  Ethical Principles
  Experimentation with Animals

■ PSYCHOLOGY IN YOUR LIFE
  Socialized Sex Differences?

B) TEXTBOOK DISCUSSION QUESTIONS

1. *In your own words, explain the conclusion of the "buyer and seller" experiment. Then provide an example of how you could apply this information to your own life. For example, a teacher who decides that he or she really wants students to work hard and may assign an enormous amount of homework. When students finally complain, the teacher reduces the workload quite a bit — which makes him or her seem flexible — yet the workload is still high, which is what the teacher wanted in the first place.*

   Examples will vary. You might want to elaborate on the "teacher" example. Students seem to like to hear about these behind-the-scenes examples.

2. *Let's say that you started off conducting an experiment on why people do not help in emergencies. Immediately after the experiment is completed, you decide to interview those people who did not help. What potential problems might you have with these interviews? Explain.*

   When confronted, people who didn't help may feel guilty about it. Consequently, these people may either outright lie about their nonhelping decisions or they may rationalize their decisions: "I didn't know it was an emergency," and so on. As discussed in the chapter, they may want to put up a favorable front.

3. *The chapter describes several methods that psychologists use in their research. If you wanted to study the effects of alcoholism on the family, which of the methods described would you use to study this and why? Explain. Briefly describe how you might conduct this research. Why would you probably not conduct your research in the laboratory?*

   Answers may vary. Interviews and the case study method would both be appropriate. One way to overcome the limitations of these methods (one limitation being that responses may not be completely honest) is to combine them with the longitudinal method. In time, family members' true intentions should surface.

   One would probably not conduct research in the laboratory because this would imply that alcohol be introduced to families as an independent variable and thus, potentially creating a problem that didn't exist in the first place.

4. *Which method of research would you probably use to study the effects of mild stress on job performance? Explain. Briefly describe how you might conduct this research.*

   A researcher would probably use a laboratory experiment. It would be simple to create a situation involving mild stress and then measuring performance. Experimenter to subjects: "The experiment is running late. You'll need to hurry."

5. *Leo is an animal rights activist. He believes we should stop all experimentation on animals and find alternative means. He argues that, if animals somehow could choose, they certainly would not choose to be part of the experiments. They suffer; they are part of the ecology; they should be given greater rights. Sam, on the other hand, believes we should experiment on animals as much as we like. He argues that only with this attitude will we ever find vaccines and cures that will improve the quality of life. He admits that animals will obviously not experience this quality life at first, but, in the long run, even they will benefit. Both of these views are extreme, but with whom do you tend to agree and why? Explain.*

Answers will obviously vary. This is a topic that you'll probably want to spend some time in class discussing. It's an interesting issue to students, and it's an important one that needs to be dealt with. One way to start a discussion is to put a scale (numbered 1-5) on the board, one end representing those who want to end all experimentation on animals, the other end representing those who feel experimentation on animals should include no limitations. Then take a poll on where they fall on the scale and discuss their reasoning. The best discussions ensue when extreme positions are presented. If you have no students who adopt these extreme positions, perhaps you can assume one yourself or assign different roles to students.

You might also have them research the role of computers in simulating the reactions of animals. (See the December 26, 1988, issue of Newsweek for a cover story on the topic.)

6. *The chapter presents the stereotype that males are better than females at video games and then explains that, if males are better, it is because they have had more practice. List three other stereotypes about sex differences; then tell whether you believe each is true and explain why or why not.*

Examples will vary. It might be fun to read these answers to the class after you pore through them.

C) TEXTBOOK ACTIVITIES

1. This activity should be fairly simple for students. However, it still may be a good idea to bring in several copies of PSYCHOLOGY TODAY and practice as a class. One way to do this is to break them up into small groups, and afterwards, have each group report back to the class. This is also a good way to familiarize them with recent research.

2. Since this is the first experiment listed in the Activity section, you'll want to make your expectations clear. Stress the need for objectivity when conducting experiments (as opposed to experimenter bias—where experimenters conduct experiments in such a way that they get the results that THEY secretly want; see part D below, #3). Stress the need for consistency: each experimental subject should be treated identically; each control subject should be treated identically. Stress the need for controlling irrelevant variables.

   MASTER 2-2 is a experiment guideline that students can use when writing their reports. If you decide to use it, you'll find that grading the reports becomes much easier. You can assign a point value to each section and simply add up the points at the end.

3. See #2 above.

4. It might be a good idea to skim through some magazines and find samples of what you consider to be good and bad surveys. Present these surveys to the class and have students discuss why a survey is good or bad.

   If students decide to do this activity, have them show you their surveys before they gather their results. Perhaps you can help them with the wording or any other problems that exist.

5. This is another set of papers that might be interesting to read aloud. If you get two or more students who adopt opposing views, maybe you can convince them to spend a few minutes debating the issue in class.

D) IN-CLASS ACTIVITIES / LESSON SUGGESTIONS

1. It should be fairly obvious that most high school students don't respond enthusiastically to the lecture method of teaching if this is the only method used in the classroom. Keep this particularly in mind when teaching Chapter 2, which includes a great deal of terminology. In fact, move this chapter along at a brisk pace. There will be ample opportunity in later chapters to reinforce the material. Instead of lecturing on this terminology, focus on the research presented in the chapter or elsewhere and apply the terminology to the research. (See part C above, #1, for ideas.)

2. Another way to reinforce the terminology in the chapter is to have the entire class conduct the experiments listed at the end of the chapter. **MASTER 2-2** is a guideline that students can use to write up their reports.

3. Conduct the following experiment on your students to demonstrate the need for objectivity and consistency when conducting experiments. *

    Materials Needed:
    Reaction-time device constructed from light cardboard (see template 1)
    Instructions
    A. Propose a hypothesis: "Males react faster than females" (if you are male), or "females react faster than males" (if you are female). This will usually elicit protests from the hypothesized "slower" sex.
    B. Define reaction time — the time interval between stimulus presentation and a subject's reaction.
    C. Select a student of the sex hypothesized as slower. Ask the student to come to the front of the room and stand with his or her hand about even with the tip of the meter, with the thumb and forefinger about two inches apart. Then, without explanation or warning, drop the meter between the subject's fingers. The subject will probably catch it. Record the reading, measuring from the top of the thumb. Reaction time is measured in centimeters here rather than seconds. Give only the one trial.
    D. Then ask for a volunteer of the opposite sex. Have this student come to the front of the room, sit down, relax, and tell you his or her preferred hand. Then define the task — to stop the meter as soon as possible when it is dropped. Hold the meter so that the point is two inches above the student's fingers (instead of even with them). Give the subject two practice trials and a verbal warning signal of

REACTION TIME METER

20 19 18 17 16 15 14 13 12 11 10 9 8 7 6 5 4 3 2 1

"ready." Then give two test trials and record only the fastest one. Then announce the "obvious conclusion" that the hypothesis has been confirmed.

E. At this point the losing sex will protest, pointing out some of the biases you introduced. List them; (a) the first student was selected, the other volunteered; (b) the first student had to use cognitive processes (since the task wasn't explained before the trial), the second student used simple reaction time; (c) the first student started with the point at fingertip level, the second started with it two inches above the fingers (leads to a discussion of the accuracy of measurement); (d) the first student had no "ready" signal, the second did; (e) the first student was standing, the second was sitting; (f) the first student had no practice, the second had practice trials.

F. Now pretend to run an unbiased test following the class suggestions. Eliminating all of the previous liases (by essentially following the procedure for the second subject), you can still easily bias the results; (a) by having a fixed foreperiod (warning-signal-to-stimulus-onset) for one subject versus a widely variable one for the other; (b) by using different motivating instructions or feedback ("That wasn't very good now, was it?"); (c) by giving one a motor set (to respond — "get ready to grab it"), which is faster than a sensory set (to observe — "watch for it to drop"); (d) by letting one subject but not the other see you "prepare" to release the stimulus.

G. Using any of the above (or in combination), your hypothesis will again be "proven." Again, have the students list the biases in this test. This may be repeated, using more subtle differences each time.

Discussion
The discussion should lead to the notion of relevant-vs-irrelevant variables in an experimental situation. Relevant variables are those likely to affect the dependent measure (reaction time), such as those used to bias this experiment. Irrelevant variables are those unlikely to affect the results, such as, in this case, barometric pressure, hair color, socioeconomic level, etc. This should lead to a discussion of the need for experimental control procedures in order to identify and control relevant variables so that both experimental conditions are the same in every regard except the independent variable. Then, any differences in results can be attributed to the independent variable.

4. Bring in "good" and "bad" surveys and discuss. (See part C above, #4.)

5. If feasible, bring your students to the school cafeteria and have a few at a time file in inconspicuously. They will jot down several naturalistic observations and attempt to draw conclusions from these observations. One problem with this sort of exercise is that hundreds of behaviors can be observed, but these behaviors may inspire, few meaningful conclusions. A way to avoid this is to provide focus for the exercise beforehand; give students something to look for. For example, what common behaviors are exhibited by large groups versus small groups? by males versus females? by freshmen versus seniors? Ask students what THEY want to focus on.

6. Ask for one male and one female volunteer to participate in a role playing activity. Take each aside separately and give them the same instructions: "You are married to __ (the other student volunteer). I am a marriage counselor, and you have come to my office because of problems in your marriage. As I interview you, I want you to present yourself in the most favorable light possible. In trying to do so, you probably don't want to attack your spouse too harshly since this will not

reflect on YOU very positively. Instead, focus on your own positive qualities." All you'll need to tell the rest of the class is that you're a marriage counselor, and that you're going to interview Mr. and Mrs. _____.

Most of your interview will be improvised since you don't know what your students will say, but here are some possible questions.
- How long have you been married? Do you both work? (and so on) —Would you say that you argue more about money or about in-laws? —Are there any personal habits of your spouse's that annoy you? —What kinds of steps do you think need to be taken to strengthen your marriage?

Here are some post-interview questions for the class.
- What did you learn about each spouse during the interview? —Which spouse did you tend to believe?
- Will the information that came out during the interview help a marriage counselor treat these spouses?
- What are some problems with using the interview method? The varied responses to the first two questions should serve to point out that one interviewer (or observer) can perceive answers differently than another. If the class doesn't mention it, point out the other major limitation of the interview method: interviewees tend to present a favorable "front" (even when NOT instructed to do so).

Last chapter, one of the lesson suggestions involved interviews between students. If you tried this activity, ask the class if any of the above limitations applied to those interviews.

7. Discuss students' attitudes on animal experimentation. (For ideas, see part 8 above, #5, and part C, #5.)

3 Body and Behavior

A. CHAPTER OUTLINE

■ THE CEREBRAL CORTEX
    The Hemispheres
    Sensory Strip
    Motor Strip
    Visual Area
    Frontal Association Area

■ THE HEMISPHERES *(in detail)*
    Handedness
    Dominance
    Tasks
    The Corpus Callosum

■ THE CEREBRAL CORTEX *(summarized)*

■ THE LOWER BRAIN
    Thalamus
    Cerebellum
    Hypothalamus
    Reticular Activating System

■ BRAIN / BODY COMMUNICATION *(Via the Nervous System)*
    Neuron
    Axon
    Dendrite
    Synapse
    Neurotransmitter
    Acetycholine
    Spinal Cord
    Reflex

■ BRAIN / BODY COMMUNICATION
(Via the Glandular or Endocrine System)
    Hormones
    Glands
        Pituitary
        Thyroid
        Adrenal
        Gonad

■ BRAIN CONTROL

B) TEXTBOOK DISCUSSION QUESTIONS

1. *Suppose you met a blind person whose corpus callosum had been cut. If you were to put a comb in this person's left hand, would he or she be able to tell you what is in his or her hand? If yes, explain. If no, what other way could the person communicate "comb" to you? Explain. What if the comb were put in his or her right hand?*

   A comb placed in a blind person's left hand is registered in only the right hemisphere (since the corpus callosum has been cut). The right hemisphere does not communicate well verbally, so this person would probably not be able to SAY comb. However, the person could probably DRAW at least a rough sketch of a comb with his or her left hand since the right hemisphere can visualize the object. Interestingly enough, if you place the pen or pencil in the same person's RIGHT hand instead, which is controlled by the left hemisphere, which does not possess any knowledge of the comb, the person will not draw a comb.

   If the comb were put into the blind person's right hand, the information goes to the left hemisphere, which does communicate well verbally, so the person would probably SAY comb.

2. *How do you suppose alcohol would affect each part of the lower brain (thalamus, hypothalamus, cerebellum, RAS) and each part of the upper brain (frontal association area, visual area, motor strip, sensory strip)? Explain.*

   Possible effects of alcohol on various parts of brain:

   Thalamus: Messages may be sent to wrong parts of body; instead of signalling the left foot to move forward, it may signal the right foot and cause the person to trip.

   Hypothalamus: The effect may vary—anger, urges of hunger and thirst.

   Cerebellum: It may disrupt coordination.

   RAS: It will probably slow down the RAS and make the person less alert and sleepy.

   The Upper Brain: In general, all parts will be dulled; complex thinking processes will be disrupted; vision may be blurred; speech may be slurred.

3. *Describe several situations where you might want your neurotransmitters to operate very efficiently and quickly. Describe several situations where you would want your neurotransmitters to work inefficiently and slowly.*

   You may want your neutrotransmitters to work inefficiently before surgery or before visiting a dentist.

   You may want your neurotransmitters to work efficiently during the performance of an important motor task, like stealing a basketball pass or saving a soccer ball from slamming into a net.

4. *The "brain transplant" is a common science fiction theme. Just for fun, imagine that the procedure has just become possible, and you have been chosen as the first candidate. Discuss the following:*
   - a. *Whose brain would you choose? Why?*
   - b. *If you had to choose between a smart, somber brain or a simple, happy brain, which would you choose? Why?*
   - c. *Regardless of your choices in (a) and (b), who would you be after the transplant? Would your identy be the same as it was before, because you would occupy the same body? Or would your identity be that of the new brain? Explain.*

   This is a question you can have fun discussing during class. Not only that, it can lead to discussion on values: "How much do you value intelligence, happiness, and so on?"

5. *Which of the three glands discussed in the chapter would probably be most affected by the aging process? Explain your reasoning and provide supporting examples. Which of the three glands would be least affected by age? Explain.*

The thyroid, which controls metabolism, would probably be most affected by age. As metabolism slows down, weight usually increases. Ask them to look at their parents now and at photos of how their parents used to look. The pituitary and adrenal glands would probably be less affected by age: growth is determined at an early age; the body's emergency system makes use of adrenaline for both the young and old. It's clear, however, that ALL the glands will be affected by age.

6. *The chapter explains that our sex drive has both physical and social aspects and that sex must be learned by humans. Other than actual experience and heart-to-heart talks, how do we learn about sex? Through TV? Through the media in general? Who or what teaches us? And what is the message being taught?*

Answers may vary. This might be an interesting question to discuss in class. Have students bring in magazine ads or song lyrics and then discuss the messages being communicated in the ads. Ask them if they believe that these kinds of messages actually have any effect on people's choices.

C) TEXTBOOK ACTIVITIES

1. This is a fun activity and the directions should be self-explanatory. You should mention to your students, however, that is impossible for an ad, or anything for that matter, to appeal to only one hemisphere. Although each hemisphere performs specialized tasks, the hemispheres don't operate isolated from each other. When a stimulus is presented, both hemispheres respond; they work together.

    You may want to tell your students to tape each ad onto a sheet of paper and to provide captions explaining why they chose the ads that they did. Also, 30 ads can become bulky; you may want to ask them to clip the ads into a folder of some sort.

2. See number 1 above.

3. Some colleges and universities (and even high schools) have portable EEG's. You might want to see if you can borrow one for a day.

4. You may want to suggest to your students that they accumulate their research not only through books, but through popular movies and novels that include scenes about lobotomies. If students DO use books for their activity (or ANY research activity), you may want to tell them to list the sources used.

5. Tell students to be creative in accumulating this information about animals. They can interview a biology teacher or a professor at a nearby university. They can contact a veterinarian or call a zoo.

6. Encourage students to invite one or two of these "knowledgeable" people to talk to the class. Another good source for speakers on drug use and abuse is a drug rehabilitation center. The staff at these centers is usually dedicated and eager to share their knowledge.

7. This research IS fascinating. Some of the articles students find may get technical and you may have to interpret.

8. See number 1 below.

D) IN-CLASS ACTIVITIES / LESSON SUGGESTIONS

1. A good way of introducing the chapter is by conducting Textbook Activity number 8 in class, using your students as subjects. There probably won't be a balance of left-handed and right-handed students, so you may need to compare males and females instead. (Don't forget to set a time for solving the puzzles.)

   Regardless of your results, this activity will serve several purposes. One, it will create immediate interest in the material. Two, it may shed light on why some people are better than others at solving these and similar kinds of puzzles. Perhaps it has nothing to do with intelligence, as many of your students may have assumed. Three, it should clarify, as suggested earlier, that the hemispheres do not operate independently from one another. They operate together.

2. An addition or an alternative to In-Class Activity number 1 is this. Pass out **MASTER 3-2** to students and again, see who performs better. This is another activity where a "balanced" brain should theoretically score higher. The left hemisphere will be primarily responsible for reading and interpreting the letters. The right hemisphere will be primarily responsible for interpreting the spatial relationship between the letters and visualizing what the incomplete word will look like with various alphabet alternatives.

   Answers to Master 3-2:

1) Statue of Liberty	6) football field
2) transportation	7) First Class Mail
3) Superman	8) The time to act is now
4) And now a word from our sponsors	9) Thanksgiving
5) Do not enter	10) Please do not feed the animals

3. At the end of the sensory and motor strip discussion early in the chapter, there is a mention about how we often "talk" to ourselves, how we can hear something in our heads without actually hearing anything. It's fairly easy and fun to demonstrate this. Pick a song that every student knows, the National Anthem, for example. Have the entire class hum the song while you direct with your hand held high. Every once in a while you will lower your hand to below your waist, but continue conducting. When you lower your hand, students should stop humming aloud, but continue humming in their brains. As you raise your hand again, students will resume humming aloud. Continue raising and lowering your hand to see if everyone can stay in unison. By the way, at least at the beginning of the song, you should probably hum aloud also. Afterwards, mention that Beethoven continued composing music even AFTER he became deaf!

4. Before discussing the specialized functions of the left and right hemispheres, post **MASTERS 3-3** and **3-4** in front of the room. Ask students which face looks happier and tally their answers. Then discuss the functions of the two hemispheres before debriefing them about the activity. Explain that most people pick face 3-3 as happier. Explanation: the question, "Which face is happier?" appeals more to the skills of the right hemisphere than the skills of the left. Why? The right hemisphere deals with emotional material. Also, the right hemisphere seems to play a special role in recognizing and interpreting faces (Schmeck, 1980). Since the appeal is primarily to the right hemisphere, the right hemisphere tends to pay special attention to the LEFT side of each picture. The left side of face 3-3 is clearly happier than the left side of face 3-4. Cover up the right side of each picture and you'll see this. (These faces aren't technically "Masters," but they're included in that section for convenience—you'll be ripping pages out of that section already.)

5. **MASTER 3-5** is an inventory that measures which hemisphere is dominant in regards to mental activity. **MASTER 3-6** is an inventory that measures which hemisphere is dominant in regards to motor activity. Point out that the way we process and remember MENTAL tasks, like remembering the multiplication tables or recalling an emotional experience, seems to be separate from the way we process and store information about MOTOR skills, like how to play the piano or how to ride a bicycle. Point out that oftentimes these MOTOR skills are so well learned that we barely need to consciously think about them. They should be able to provide numerous examples of this: throwing a ball, running, even walking to class. This should explain why musicians and athletes need to practice and drill over and over again. They're training not only their minds but their bodies as well. This is not to suggest, of course, that processing mental skills remains independent of the processing of motor skills. One obviously affects the other. For example, many athletes maintain that simply visualizing a drill does almost as much good as performing the drill.

After students fill out Master 3-6 (Hemisphere Dominance Inventory for Motor Skills), tell them to add the number of left and right answers. Their tally should provide them with a rough idea of their hemisphere dominance for motor skills. The more right answers they have, the more dominant their left hemisphere, and vice-versa. (Instead of having students fill out the inventory silently, you may want to go over each question as a class and have students act out the motor skills using BOTH sides of their bodies!)

The following is an analysis you can use for **MASTER 3-5**, the questionnaire for mental dominance. Of course, you can find more extensive tests of this sort quite easily if you're interested.

ANALYSIS FOR LEFT-HEMISPHERE DOMINANCE (left-hemisphere total = 10 or more.)

Your score indicates that you are generally a highly organized person. If you are a sloppy person, even your mess makes sense to you. When given a job to do, you like to approach the task one step at a time rather than plunging into it. If you're involved in extra-curricular activities, you're probably well disciplined. For example, if you're a musician, you usually have no problem sticking to a schedule. In the future, you'd probably do well in one of the following areas: accounting, math, engineering or computer programming.

ANALYSIS FOR RIGHT-HEMISPHERE DOMINANCE (Right-hemisphere total = 10 or more.)

Your score indicates that you use intuition and creativity in order to achieve certain goals, rather than an outlined, detailed plan of action. You feel that too much planning tends to limit possibilities. If you're involved in an extracurricular activity that requires practice or drilling, like concert band or a team, you perform well when inspired, but otherwise you don't enjoy the routine of practicing every day. Chances are good that you're interested in one of the following areas: music, art, athletics.

ANALYSIS FOR BALANCE HEMISPHERES (Both totals = less than 10.)

As indicated in the previous descriptions, "left-hemisphere people" prefer structure environments, whereas "right-hemisphere people" prefer unstructured environments. Your score indicates that you fall somewhere between these two extremes. When given a job to do, you may prepare yourself by making lists, for example (something a left-hemisphere person would do), but the lists themselves may not be highly structured (this loose structure being something a right-hemisphere person would prefer).

6. Most of the information here and in the chapter about the functions of the left and right hemispheres has been mainly theoretical. Here are two practical applications.

A) Oftentimes, when students take notes, they condense what should be seven pages of lecture information into a single page. Some of them must have nightmares of paper shortage. When students condense their notes, they create few, if any, spatial relationships between one section and another. Therefore, when they take notes, when they study notes, and when they try to recall notes during tests, they rely only on verbal skills, the strength of the left hemisphere. Solution: simply tell students to space out their notes to CREATE spatial relationships. Point out how common it is while taking a test to know WHERE the information is located in one's notebook. These location cues are desirable as they often prompt a more specific recall of the material. Intentionally spacing out lecture material helps to create a greater number of these location cues in which the right hemisphere specializes. In other words, both hemispheres will be used more efficiently.

B) When delivering a lecture and writing notes on the board, make it a point to draw simple pictures or diagrams whenever possible. For example, when discussing the cerebellum, you might draw a person balancing on a tightrope. Or when discussing the hypothalamus, you can draw a glass of water or a hamburger. If you can't think of a picture, maybe your students can. And don't worry about artistic ability—the worse, the better. Once you start drawing pictures on the blackboard, you can be assured that most students will also copy them into their notebooks. Explain that these pictures will also help create location cues which will appeal to the skills of the right hemisphere.

4 Sensation and Perception

A. CHAPTER OUTLINE

■ SENSATION
Vision
    Light
    Structure of the eye
        Cornea, Lens, Pupil, Retina, Blind Spot
    Receptors in the Retina
    Rods and Cones
    Color Vision
    Color Defects
    Afterimages
Hearing *(Audition)*
    Pitch, Intensity, Decibels
    Structure of the Ear
        Eardrum, Cochlea, Hair Cells, Auditory Nerve
Cutaneous Senses
Smell
    Mechanisms of Smell
    Smell Communication
Taste
    Salt Needs
    Bitterness Needs
    Sugar Needs

■ PERCEPTION
Perceptual Constancies
    Size Constancy
    Color Constancy
    Brightness Constancy
    Space Constancy
Depth Perception
    Visual Cliff
    Binocular Disparity
    Visual Texture
Similarity
Closure
Illusions
Reversible Figure
Subliminal Perception
ESP

B) TEXTBOOK DISCUSSION QUESTIONS

1. *Briefly define ultraviolet and infrared wavelengths. Describe how the world might be different if humans had receptors for these wavelengths. Be specific.*

   Ultraviolet wavelengths are too slow for our eyes. Infrared wavelengths are too fast for our eyes. If humans had receptors for UV wavelengths, they would probably see flowers and plants very differently. The plants might look more like a series of patterns. Humans might also be able to see a deeper blue and a deeper purple (which students may not surmise from information in the text). If humans had receptors for infrared wavelengths, they could probably function better in the dark. Again, students may not surmise this, but humans would probably see heat in a different way. For example, a pot of boiling water might glow. Or one might actually see the heat off the highway.

2. *Which of your senses is most important to you? Explain. If you had to give up one sense, which one would you give up? Why? What if you had to choose between giving up hearing and giving up seeing?*

   Answers will vary. You may want to discuss this one in class.

3. *What if you could magically improve the performance of one of your senses? Which sense would you choose to improve? Why? Could you improve the performance of one sense without magic? How? Be specific.*

   Those who meditate on a regular basis often report a keener and richer awareness of the world. Whether this improves the "performance" of their senses is probably more questionable. Those who lose the use of one sense, blind people for instance, often report that their other senses become stronger.

4. *If we compare the performance of our senses as human beings to the senses of other animals, what conclusions can we draw? Do humans rate poorly, average, or above average? Why? Explain.*

   In comparing human sensation to animal sensation, humans probably rate average or below average. Students should be able to cite several examples from their own experiences and from the chapter. For example, bees use ultraviolet light to find flowers, and snakes use infrared light, wereas humans can use neither of these. Dolphins and bats use sound waves in ways that humans will never experience.

5. *Each day our senses are bombarded with stimulation from the environment. What do you suppose would happen if we were completely deprived of this stimulation for two or three days? List several possible side effects. Hint: Try finding someone who has driven alone on the highway at night; how did the person feel once fatigue set in?*

   Experiments performed in the 50's reveal that subjects often experience mild hallucinations after 2-3 days of sensory deprivation. It seems that when the brain is deprived of stimulation, it creates its own. If you've ever driven long distances, especially at night, you've probably experienced this hallucinatory type of stimulation: shadowy creatures dart in front of the car; traffic signs become hitchhikers; viaducts become huge trucks.

6. *The chapter explains that ESP may be an extra sense. Do you think human beings have any other extra senses? To answer this question, you might research kinesthesis, circadian rhythms, and equilibratory senses.*

   Kinesthesis gives us feedback about our muscles and joints and tendons. If we close our eyes and walk, we can still sense one foot in front of the other. Circadian rhythm refers to the internal, natural clock of the body. (See Chapter 6.) Equilibratory senses inform a person where his or her body is in space. Carnival rides tend to disrupt these equilibratory senses.

7. *Assume you are an experimental psychologist. Someone who claims to have ESP asks for an appointment with you in your laboratory. What kinds of questions would you ask? What types of experiments would you conduct?*

Have students refer back to the scientific method section described in Chapter 2. An experimental psychologist would want to conduct experiments in an objective manner that would allow the possibility of replicating the experiment in the future. Also, the experimenter would want to include tight controls. Mention to students that the study of ESP has been marred by sloppy experimental procedures. It seems that many ESP researchers are so eager to find evidence of ESP that they become guilty of experimenter bias. See the March 1983 issure of DISCOVER MAGAZINE for ideas.

8. *Do you think that subliminal messages have any influence on people? Explain. Assume that these messages do influence people in some way; should the messages be regulated by law? Do you see any dangers in their use?*

Answers will vary. See the September 1988 issue of PSYCHOLOGY TODAY for ideas.

C) TEXTBOOK ACTIVITIES

1. This is an activity you may want to conduct in class.

2. If given a choice of activities to do, most students will not choose this one. If you really want a blind speaker to talk to your class, you'll probably need to specifically assign someone to call a center for the blind.

3. The creative writers in your classes should enjoy this one. Read the best ones in class and get permission to photocopy these so you can read them to future classes.

4. This is another activity you may want to discuss in class BEFORE students get a chance to read the activity.

   "Which hemisphere should play a greater role in solving the illusion?" In order to create the illusion, one would need to rely on spatial skills, mentally bending and turning the paper over — a specialization of the right hemisphere. Most people, however, probably try to be analytical, wondering what the "trick" is—a task in which the left hemisphere probably specializes.

5. The setting for conducting the experiment should be discussed. If the psychology enrollment at your school is high, nonpsychology students may learn of the purpose of the experiment through overexposure. Ideally, the experiment should be conducted at a grocery store where these kinds of tests are expected. If students DO conduct the experiment in school, perhaps they can claim that the test is for another course, Consumer Education, or Food 101, for example.

6. To set up this activity, you might want to discuss the psychology of color (which colors make us hungry? and so on). Either have students research the topic or do it yourself and report the findings. Popular magazines and local newspapeers often run reports on this topic. Just be wary of the conclusions. Were they gotten throught scientific research?

7. Students should enjoy this one. If it's feasible, you may want to bring your class to the cafeteria and have students conduct the experiment during the first half of the class period. The second half can be used to tally and discuss the results.

D) IN-CLASS ACTIVITIES / LESSON SUGGESTIONS

1. In addition to conducting a taste test in class, as suggested earlier, conduct a touch test. Bring to class 7-10 lemons or potatoes or whatever else is on sale. Also bring in 10 blindfolds. If you cut an old sheet into small strips, you'll have more blindfolds than a magician. With a marker, number each lemon.

    Have ten students volunteer to sit in a circle on the floor. Have them put on a blindfold. Give each of them a lemon and tell them the number. Allow them about a minute to "get to know" their lemons. After this one minute, collect all the lemons and randomly give back a lemon to each student. Still blindfolded, they will pass lemons around the circle, attempting to find their assigned lemons.

    Most students doubt that they will be able to find their original lemons. This activity should demonstrate how well developed our senses are. Have fun varying the above procedure to test the limits of the senses. For example, each person can examine two lemons rather than one, or the time limit can be shortened, and so on.

2. This next activity is a variation of #1. Have students pair up with a partner. Give each pair one blindfold and whatever hall pass students may need to walk around the building. Allow them about 20 minutes to quietly walk around the building. This will allow each person about 10 minutes to walk around blindfolded and 10 minutes to be a guide.

    Tasks for the blindfolded partner: a)walk down stairs; b)walk backwards; c)drink from a water fountain; d)find a place to sit down. Brainstorm with your class for other tasks.

    Tasks for the "guide" (not blindfolded): a)ensure the safety of the blindfolded partner; b)say as little as possible.

    When students return to class, discuss their reactions. What tasks were harder than they thought? Easier than they thought? Did they develop a sense of trust or distrust for the guide? They were only blindfolded for 10 minutes, but did their other senses seem to become more alert at all? Before conducting this discussion, you may have students write a journal entry about their reactions. Ten minutes should be enough time for this. Having them write down their reactions may elicit more thoughtful responses to the activity.

    If you're reluctant to try this activity because you're afraid that the introverted students won't participate, you may be surprised. Even the most withdrawn students seem to enjoy this.

3. Read **MASTER 4-2**. It's an activity for your students, but before giving it to them, conduct the activity in class using an opaque projector. If an opaque projector is unavailable, simply walk around and show the picture. Show half the class picture "A." Show the other half picture "B." Then show picture "C" to the entire class.

    This activity can lead to a discussion on how "set" can influence attitudes. For example, when depressed, we view the world through a set frame of mind: "No one likes me; life will never get better; I'm no good." Everything is viewed as an absolute with little gray area. When depressed, we find it difficult to break out of this absolute set, just as we initially find it difficult to see an old woman in the picture if we have been set up to see the young woman, and vice-versa. In other words, we may become depressed, or stay depressed, in part, because of our thoughts—which is exactly what cognitive psychologists believe (see Chapter 1).

4. The text includes numerous illustrations of similarity, illusions, and so on. However, there are only so many illustrations that any text can include. Since viewing these kinds of illustrations is of high interest to students, obtain a set of these illustrations to display in class. Museums often sell these kinds of illustrations. Or perhaps your library has a book by M.C. Escher whose bizarre sketches qualify as illusions. Or see section 2 or this manual for ideas on where to order the above.

5. Skim through any magazines that include numerous colorful ads and rip out several of them. If you study them closely, you'll often find subliminal messages embedded in the ice cubes or the hair or somewhere else in the ad. If you can find any of these subliminal messages, point these out to your class. Despite the lack of hard evidence that subliminal messages influence behavior, advertisers definitely insert these messages in their ads—just in case.

6. This activity is wild and perhaps not for everyone, but it can be one of the highlights of the class, one of those activities that through word of mouth boosts enrollment in Psychology. Examine **MASTER 4-3** and you'll notice several "3's" subliminally embedded in each rectangle. Photocopy this Master several times, cut out the rectangles, and you'll have 16-20 index-sized cards. With a bright marker, write a question on each card. The content of these questions will become clear as you read on.

Use the cards to conduct a "Dating Game" experiment! You need 3 males or 3 females from your class to volunteer as contestants, and you need one person, the opposite sex of your contestants, from outside of your class (from the cafeteria or study hall) to volunteer. Set up some kind of barrier between the 3 contestants and the subject. A barrier is easily created by taping a long, wide strip of paper to the top of a podium and placing the podium on your desk. The subject will read the questions you have written on the cards; the contestants will answer them as well as they can. After asking all the questions, the subject will choose one of the contestants. (Have fun with this procedure: announce where the subject and lucky contestant will go on their date; present a commercial while the subject is deciding whom to choose; include music; and so on.) The purpose of the "experiment" is to see if the subject will be influenced by the "3's" on the cards.

By now, you have certainly noticed several major flaws in The Dating Game "experiment." The real purpose of the experiment is to evoke discussion about sublimanal perception and about experimental design.

When introducing the activity to students, stress how you're going to try to be as scientific as possible. Show them the cards (not your questions); create a simple data sheet on which someone will record the number of times the subject looks at the subliminal cards and how many seconds the subject looks at the cards; be sure to find a subject who does not know the contestants (when finding the subject, bring a list of names, three of which— the contestants—the subject must not know). Despite your emphasis on being scientific, many students will still identify many flaws in the "experiment," which is fine, but tell them to save their comments until after the game.

Once the game is over, have students make a list of the flaws in the experiment: 1)There was no control group; some cards should not have included ANY subliminal messages; 2) More subjects should have been tested; 3) The contestants' answers should have been essentially the same; even the voice patterns should have been close to identical; 4) There shouldn't have been an audience; perhaps the audience was biased and influenced the subject. Students should be able to think of several other flaws.

Once you have exhausted this discussion, discuss the feasibility of eliminating these flaws. Then, assuming that these flaws have been eliminated, and assuming that subliminal messages do influence subjects' choices, should we allow subliminal messages to be used in the real world? By advertisers? By employers? By school administrators?

Possible questions to include on the cards: 1) If you could be any animal in the world, which one would you be and why? 2) If you had one wish, what would it be and why? 3) What is one thing that really annoys you? 4) To what kinds of places do you like to go on a first date? (A final note: if you want, you can easily squeeze in two games in one class period.)

7. Read **MASTERS 4-4** and **4-5**. If you want to try this one on your students, pass out the Masters face down and have students fold the sheets in half so they cannot read the instructions at the bottom. Otherwise, just hand them out to students as an extra activity.

8. One of the biggest criticisms of parapsychological (ESP) research is that experimenters are so eager to find someone with ESP that their experiements are sloppily controlled. This next activity should demonstrate that most of us are eager to believe; also, it should point out the need for tighter controls.

   Procedure: Explain to students that you know someone who has ESP (an uncle or aunt, and so on). Tell an amazing story or two about this person. Explain that this "psychic" has agreed to try a little experiment with your class. Explain that the psychic is at home waiting to guess the identity of a playing card that the class will randomly pick. Have the class "pick a card, any card." Then take 3 students with you to a phone and call the psychic. Put the phone next to your students' ears and the "psychic" will identify the correct card!

   When you get back to class, have the 3 amazed students describe to the class exactly what happened. The rest of the class will usually have a great deal of questions about the psychic's ability. You can recount another amazing story or two. If you know any other appropriate magic tricks, perform them, claiming that your psychic friend taught you how to get in touch with your own ESP. You can keep your secret a while longer, but you shoud reveal your true intentions by the end of the class.

   Apologize for duping them and explain why you did it: A) to show how eager we all are to believe in ESP: B) to demonstrate the need for tighter controls; you can discuss how your phone exercise is unscientific (this is something you can discuss even before revealing your secret); C) to demonstrate the power of labels --just because you labeled someone a psychic, their expectations followed suit (so to speak). Throughout all this it's important to emphasize that you're not trying to discredit the existence of ESP; you're not trying to convince them NOT to believe in ESP. It's just that the study of ESP needs to be conducted scientifically to gain credibility amongst scientists.

   By the way, this is how to do the phone trick. Your friend needs to know WHEN you're going to phone. Dial the friend's number. The friend will answer, immediately reciting, "Ace, two, three," and so on. In the meantime, you haven't said a word. You're still waiting for someone to answer the phone! When your friend says your number, you say, "Hello, is —home?" Your friend will then recite, "hearts, diamonds, clubs, spades." When the friend reaches your suit, you say, "Hold on." The friend now knows the exact card. Hand the phone over to your students and have them say, "Hello." Simple!

5 Motivation and Emotion

A. CHAPTER OUTLINE

■ PHYSICAL FACTORS OF MOTIVATION AND EMOTION

Hypothalamus
Reticular Formation
Pituitary Gland
Adrenal Gland
Gonads
    Androgen
    Estrogen

■ MOTIVATION

Hunger
    Causes of Hunger
    Factors Controlling Weight

Thirst

Psychological Needs
    Curiosity Motives
    Manipulation Motive

Intrinsic vs. Extrinsic Motivation
Need for Stimulation
Maslow's Hierarchy Theory of Motivation

■ EMOTIONS

Cognition

Theories of Emotion
    James Lange Theory
    Cannon-Bard Theory
    Schachter's Congnitive Theory

B) TEXTBOOK DISCUSSION QUESTIONS

1. *The chapter mentions that eating is a special ritual. Analyze your own family meals, taking into account both past and present gatherings. What "rituals" does your family seem to follow? What do these rituals say about your family? Have the rituals changed over the years? What does this say about your family?*

   This is a fun issue to discuss in class, especially if your students represent a wide range of ethnic backgrounds.

2. *Do you think that, in general, motivation changes as you get older? If so, in what ways does it change? Be specific. If not, provide examples to show that motivation does not change.*

   If you discuss this question in class, break it down into categories. A) How do developmental changes affect motivation? As one becomes older, metabolism slows down. Perhaps the motivation to exercise then becomes greater—maybe. B) How do interpersonal changes affect motivation? For example, does marriage increase or decrease the need for safety? C) How do career choices affect motivation?

3. *Imagine that your parents gave you $100 for each A that you received on your report card. First, do you think that the money would motivate you? Why or why not? Second, assume that the money did motivate you. Would you actually learn more? Why or why not?*

   Answers will vary. You may find that some of your students' parents DO pay cash for grades. Ask THESE students if the cash is motivational?

4. *Besides money, what motivates your parent(s) to go to work every day? Explain. Which motivators are more important-money or the ones you've just listed? Explain.*

   Answers will vary. Most answers will fit somewhere on Maslow's hierarchy of needs. Relating their answers to Maslow's theory should provide an effective summary.

5. *Briefly define extrinsic and intrinsic motivation. Then analyze Maslow's theory and decide which of his hierarchy needs are extrinsically satisfied, which are intrinsically satisfied, and which, if any, are satisfied in both ways. Explain.*

   Physiological and safety needs are extrinsically satisfied for the most part. Food and water and houses are examples. Belongingness, self-esteem, and self-actualization needs are intrinsically satisfied for the most part. For example, if we enroll in a course, it's safe to assume that we "belong" in that course, yet for various reasons we may not always FEEL as if we belong. We need to intrinsically decide that we belong; our enrollment registration card (an extrinsic symbol) may be insufficient.

   You can probably think of several exceptions to the above. For example, someone may extrinsically satisfy his or her safety needs by installing seventeen dead bolt locks on the doors of his or her house, yet this person may still FEEL unsafe.

6. *Compare Maslow's hierarchy of needs to your own life. Which needs have you adequately satisfied? Explain. (If you have indeed satisfied these needs, you don't spend much time thinking about them.) Which needs are you currently tying to satisfy? Explain. (These are needs that you do spend a great deal of time thinking about.)*

    Answers will vary.

7. *According to Maslow, self-actualizers are people who strive to do their best, strive to reach their potential. If you look around, you'll probably agree that very few people consistently choose this path. Why not? Offer several reasons or explanations.*

    Answers will vary. Many do not strive to do their best because they haven't satisfied the lower levels in Maslow's hierarchy. Or perhaps some people don't strive to do their best because then the best will be expected in the future. It's easier to be average.

8. *Think of a time when someone rejected you (for a job, a date, a favor, whatever). Which of the theories of emotions best describes how you felt after the rejection? Explain.*

    Answers will vary.

C) TEXTBOOK ACTIVITIES

1. To prepare students for this activity, you might have each student find an article about dieting methods and follow this up with a class discussion. Do the diets try to curb the influence of external cues? What do the diets suggest people do about internal cues? Do diet plans work? The few students who have tried different diets may not be willing to discuss their experiences, but they and others may be willing to discuss their parents' diets.

2. Contacting a fast food restaurant is optional and requires extra effort by students. As you know, most students are unwilling to DO extra, so you may want to provide incentive for this part of the activity. Extra credit? No homework for one night? Your lifelong bond of friendship?

3. Before assigning this activity, bring in several ads and analyze them according to the instructions in the activity. Some students may need this practice in order to properly complete the activity.

4. See #3 above.

5. This is a good one to discuss in class after students have completed the assignment. Or you may want to actually conduct this activity in class yourself. Simply bring into class several ads and a radio. This kind of on-the-spot, "live" analysis often makes class time dynamic and exciting.

6. Collages are often difficult to grade. Before assigning this activity, choose the criteria you will use to grade them and explain these criteria to your students. General criteria may include effort, thought, organization, and neatness. Also, arrange your criteria in order of importance.

7. Anorexia nervosa and bulimia can be sensitive issues for high school students. Assure students that any personal information included in their reports will remain confidential. This is not to suggest that you should avoid discussing these issues in class. Such a discussion can be very worthwhile.

D) IN-CLASS ACTIVITIES / LESSON SUGGESTIONS

1. Discussion question #1 asks students to analyze their families' eating rituals. It might be fun to discuss not only this issue in class, but to discuss the eating rituals students follow amongst friends. For example, when they meet at a fast food restaurant, what kinds of "rules" apply? "Must" they play with straws? Are napkins used as napkins, or do they serve another purpose? What kinds of "uniforms" are worn? Ask them to compare and contrast these rituals with rituals followed at other kinds of restaurants. Finally, ask if all these "rules" change as one grows older. In other words, in what ways, if any, do freshmen rituals differ from junior or senior rituals?

2. Discussion question #2 asks students whether motivation changes as one gets older. To find out, ask students to make a list of several motivations they have for coming to school. At the same time, send three or four students around the school to ask teachers and administrators the same question. When both lists are completed, compare and contrast the two. Is one list more self-centered than the other? Is one more materialistic than the other?

3. To demonstrate the curiosity motive, simply perform a "curious" behavior or task—without explanation—and mentally note students' curious reactions. For example, put a student's desk on your desk, leave it alone, and begin lecturing. If the students are NOT curious, continue lecturing for a short while, then perform another curious behavior. Continue this procedure until their curiosity interferes with your lecture (and if this doesn't happen, take their pulses), then discuss their curious reactions. How and when did they express their curiosity? What factors inhibited them from expressing their curiosity? Does school in general promote or stifle our curiosity motive?

4. Pass out **MASTER 5-2** before discussing or having students read about Maslow's hierarchy needs. Present this scenario: "You are shipwrecked alone on a desert island. Which of the five needs listed in the middle of the sheet would you need to satisfy first? After satisfying this need, which need would you satisfy next? And so on?" Have students write #1 next to the first need they would satisfy, a #2 next to the second need, and so on. Once they've completed this arrangement, discuss their choices. Then briefly explain Maslow's order and have them insert each need into its respective level on the pyramid. (If their previous arrangement of the needs differs from Maslow's order, have them scratch this to avoid confusion.)

   Finally, have them match the adjectives at the bottom of the sheet with Maslow's needs. Discuss and correct their answers. This activity should help clarify the logic of the order of the hierarchy.

Answers to Matching:

rest	1	sensory stimulation	1
political security	2	economic security	2
love	3	skill strength	4
food	1	affection	3
power	4	oxygen	1
water	1	independence	4
exercise	1	temperature control	1
self-confidence	4	accurate perception of self	5
fulfillment of potential	5	living quarters	2
feeling worthwhile	4		

5. If you check with your audiovisual department or school library, you may find that your school owns or can rent a film that includes a series of television commercials. Show the film (or video) to your class. After each commercial, have students jot down which of Maslow's hierarchy needs the product in the commercial satisfies and the need to which the ad appeals (similar to textbook Activity #3). It's probably a good idea to show a few commercials at a time and then discuss each one rather than waiting until the very end for discussion; it's easy to forget the details of the commercials.

6. To further clarify Maslow's hierarchy, you might simply ask students HOW they satisfy or have satisfied each of the five levels. For example, one's safety need might be satisfied by locking doors at night, covering windows with steel bars, installing an alarm system. Note that the above provide primarily PHYSICAL safety. This physical safety may lead to a sense of PSYCHOLOGI-CAL safety, but we achieve this psychological safety in other ways as well: insurance; bank accounts; long-term commitments (marriage); employment contracts.

   Once you've exhausted this discussion, break the class into small groups. Each group will try to think of two or three famous people or organizations (or whatever) that operate almost exclusively at one of Maslow's five levels. For example, for level one, students might include poor people who don't know when their next meal will come. For level two, students might include the homeless, and so on. Students' choices are often original and creative. Have them provide brief reasons for their choices. Almost any choice is acceptable if the reasoning is in line with Maslow's theory.

7. This activity is not for the meek. Think of a way to mildly scare at least several students in your classroom. Perhaps you can have someone charge into class crashing cymbals. Or if you can get a loud cap gun that track and field officials use, perhaps you can sound it off in class unexpectedly. Or inconspicuously release a wind-up spider that races madly around the room (novelty shops often sell such items). Be creative. If you're willing to try this first part, the second part will be worthwhile. After you've scared several students, analyze their emotions. Discuss which of the three theories of emotions best explains their reactions.

6 States of Consciousness

A. CHAPTER OUTLINE

- DEFINING CONSCIOUSNESS
    - Making a Mental Map
    - Levels of Consciousness

- CHRONOBIOLOGY
    - Biological Clocks
        - Entrainment
        - Circadian Rhythms
        - Fighting the Clock
        - Giving up Sleep

- SLEEP AND DREAMS
    - REM Sleep
    - Brain Changes During Sleep
        - Alpha, Beta, and Delta Waves
    - NREM Sleep
    - Purpose of Dreaming

- PSYCHOLOGY OF DREAMS
    - Dream Content
    - Nightmares
    - Incubus Attacks

- PRACTICAL ISSUES IN SLEEP
    - Social Entrainment
    - Length of Sleep

- WALKING AND TALKING IN SLEEP
    - Sleep Disturbances
        - Insomnia
        - Narcolepsy
        - Sleep Apnea

- HYPNOSIS
    - Nature of Hypnosis
    - Special State?
        - Trance
    - Uses of Hypnosis

- MEDITATION

B) TEXTBOOK DISCUSSION QUESTIONS

1. *Besides consciousness, can you think of any other constructs, or beliefs, that people have? List one. (Remember, a construct can't be seen or touched.) What evidence would suggest that this construct actually exists?*

   Any abstract concepts like love, hate, envy, and so on, are acceptable answers.

2. *Consciousness is an awareness of what is going on inside and outside the organism. Do you think that people who are highly intelligent experience this awareness at a greater level than people who are less intelligent? Explain.*

   A greater level of awareness is probably more related to motivation and sensitivity and open-mindedness than intelligence. On the other hand, one's level of awareness could probably not be great without a certain degree of cognitive development. In other words, an adult would probably possess a greater level of awareness than a child.

3. *The unconscious contains thoughts and desires about which we have no knowledge. If you could suddenly become aware of these "hidden" thoughts by simply pushing a button, would you do it? Why or why not?*

4. *If you could completely give up sleep without many physical side effects, would you do it? Why or why not? Remember, no sleep means no dreaming.*

5. *Do you consider yourself a long sleeper or a short sleep? If you're a long sleeper, how do you feel when you can only sleep a short time? Explain. If you're a short sleeper, how do you feel when you've had too much sleep? Explain.*

6. *Since dogs and cats have REM, it's probably safe to assume that they "dream." What would you guess makes up the content of their "dreams"? Explain.*

7. *With which of the three major theories that explain why we dream do you most agree? Explain.*

8. *If you could automatically remember and control all your dreams, would you want this ability? Why or why not?*

   Answers: 3, 4, 5, 6, 7, 8
   The answers to all these questions (3, 4, 5, 7, 8) will vary. These are the kinds of questions that should provide lively discussions in class. If you DO discuss these questions in class, point out from time to time how their answers may reflect their values and/or personality.

   If your students enjoy role-playing, question #6 should provide a unique opportunity. Students can assume the roles of animals who reveal the content of their dreams by talking in their sleep.

9. *In general, do you believe that you could be hypnotized? Why or why not?*

   People who do not believe that they can be hypnotized probably never will be. A "good" hypnosis subject will believe, will be eager to follow the suggestions of the hypnotist, and will usually be highly imaginative. Perhaps you can compare students' attitudes about dreams to their answers to this question. Those same students who view dreaming as mystical and highly meaningful are probably the same students who believe that they can be hypnotized.

C) TEXTBOOK ACTIVITIES

1. The text includes four good interview questions, but you may insist that students write several of their own questions as well.

2. As with question #1, you may want students to add their own questions to the ones already listed in the text.

   Something to think about: If you have 100 students, and you have each student survey 30 subjects, you'll possess a great deal of data upon which to draw conclusions! To make this tallying of data more exciting, design a poster-board data chart, post it in class, and have each student orally report his or her results while you fill in the chart. The survey is so short that this tallying will only take five or ten minutes per class. Then you can analyze and discuss these results as a class, or you can have each student write his or her own analysis based upon your chart.

3. Definitely insist that students add their own survey questions to the ones already listed in the text. See #2 above for additional suggestions.

4. See #2 and #3 above.

5. See #1 and #2 in Section D.

6. These kinds of reports aren't the most exciting to read and grade, but some students prefer this kind of activity over surveys and interviews. Just insist that students use their own words to avoid plagiarism.

7. Be sure to have students hand in the drawing, the two dream paragraphs, and their comparative analyses—otherwise, grading this activity may be difficult; you may not understand the logic of their conclusions.

D) IN-CLASS ACTIVITIES / LESSON SUGGESTIONS

1. Most students look forward to this chapter because it includes a section on dreams. Allow them an outlet to express their enthusiasm by conducting an informal discussion on dreams at the very beginning of the unit. Possible discussion questions: "Describe some memorable dreams that you've had. What do you think these dreams mean? In general, what do you think is the purpose of dreaming? What is the purpose of nightmares? Can you sometimes control your dreams?" Other ideas: Ask them the survey questions in textbook Activity #3. Recount some of your own memorable dreams and what they mean to you. Allow them to ask questions. Even if you cannot provide the answers to all their questions, you create a healthy inquisitiveness. Perhaps you can assign students to find the answers to these unanswered questions. Or maybe you can invite an expert to class (a therapist who analyzes dreams to treat patients, and so on) to answer questions. (One question invariably asked is, "Can you die in your dreams?" Myth says that you can't. Although it's rare—even in dreams you tend to protect yourself—it IS possible to die in your dreams.)

2. If you want students to keep a dream journal, you need to allow them a couple of weeks to complete and analyze it. The biggest problem that students have is remembering their dreams or remembering to write down the dreams they do remember. You can help to alleviate this problem in two ways: 1) Have an informal discussion on dreams at the very beginning of the unit (see #1 above); 2) Have students keep a "day journal" in class during the course of the consciousness unit. Each day or every other day, assign a topic in class and allow students about ten minutes to freely respond to the topic. Possible topics:

   a) Describe an ideal place that you'd like to be NOW.
   b) You're in a plane. You're flying through bad weather. You're worried that you're going to crash. Write a letter to someone.
   c) Describe a date from the point of view of someone of the opposite sex.
   d) Describe someone chasing you. You don't know this person. By the end of your entry resolve the chase somehow. (Afterwards, ask who this person most resembles in real life?)
   e) Think about one of the biggest regrets of your life. Go back. Describe how you wish things would have turned out.
   f) Describe your thirtieth birthday. Where will you be? What will you be? With whom will you be?
   g) Besides acquiring money and starting a career, describe one of your biggest dreams or goals. Describe how you'll feel when you achieve your dream.
   h) Everyone has problems or troubling concerns. Write about one of your biggest current problems. Describe how your life will be when you resolve this problem.
   i) Describe a happy or proud experience in your life.
   j) Post a photograph or picture on the board. Have students respond to the picture.

Notice that many of these topics are similar to common themes in dreams. The idea is for students, during the day, to write down their conscious observations about these kinds of themes. Then in the morning, when they jot down their dreams, they will write down their "unconscious" observations of these or other dream themes. The hope is that at some time, the two journals will intersect somehow and provide students with some insights. If this is too ambitious, the day journal at least serves as a reminder to write down their dreams.

MASTER 6-2 is an assignment sheet for students explaining all of the above. Make clear that you will not read any journal entries that are marked "Personal." In fact, you may suggest that they rip out these pages, allow you to glance at them as proof of completion, and then NOT hand them in. If during the course of this assignment you realize that some students just cannot remember their dreams, you might suggest that they write more day journal entries and write a written report based on this day journal.

This is obviously not necessary, but it's a good idea to keep your own dream journal at the same time that your students do. You'll better understand some of the frustration students may experience in remembering their dreams. And you may develop insights into how to remember dreams or how to interpret them (although there is no single, correct method).

3. This activity works better if combined with #1 and #2 above, but it can be used alone as well. Bring in construction paper and several boxes of crayons and spread all this on the floor. Tell students to recall a particularly vivid dream that they have had recently. It's best to choose a dream that seems MEANINGFUL to them as well. Once they all have a dream in mind, have them choose paper and crayons to draw the dream. When the drawings are completed, have them sit in a circle and tape the pictures to the front of their desks so everyone can see them. Each student will briefly explain the details of his or her dream WITHOUT providing any possible interpretations. After this brief explanation, the rest of the class will try to analyze the drawing. What colors does the person use? How intense are the lines? How do these factors relate to the content?

    Explain that you're not searching for correct answers. If students treat this activity seriously (and they usually do and they enjoy it), it can lead to a worthwhile discussion on the purpose of dreams and dream content.

4. When discussing REM sleep, have students look at a partner. The partner should close his or her eyes and rapidly look left and right over and over again. Students won't forget what REM stands for.

5. This is a simple activity to demonstrate that hypnosis is not as mystical as it seems. Have students put out their hands straight in front of them, palms down. Tell them to look at their hands and then close their eyes. Then suggest, over and over, that their hands are sinking down, lower and lower. Recite these instructions very slowly and rhythmically. After a minute or two, several hands WILL sink down. Have them open their eyes and many of them will be amazed. This should demonstrate the power of a simple suggestion.

6. Most American students have little or no experience with meditation. If you'd like to expand their horizons a bit, obtain a copy of a meditation cassette tape, play it in class, and allow students to meditate for fifteen to twenty minutes. A good tape will usually provide step-by-step instructions about body position, and so on. To create a proper atmosphere, turn off the lights and have students spread out by themselves on the floor. If possible, eliminate any possibly distractions or interruptions from outside the classroom: tape paper over any glass in the door so people can't look in, and so on.

    Afterwards, discuss the difficulties they had in following the instructions on the tape. They surely will not experience many benefits after only fifteen or twenty minutes, but perhaps they can guess what benefits they would experience if they meditated on a daily basis. Assuming that these benefits WILL be experienced, ask why students do not meditate. (The benefits aren't that valued; society doesn't promote it, and so on.)

7 Cognitive Processes

A. CHAPTER OUTLINE

■ CLASSICAL CONDITIONING
    Ivan Pavlov's Experiments
    Classical Conditioning Procedure or "Formula"
    John Watson's Experiments with Little Albert
        Stimulus Generalization
    Mary Cover Jones and Peter
        Removal of Fears

■ OPERANT CONDITIONING
    B.F. Skinner
    Reinforcement
        Primary Reinforcement
        Secondary Reinforcement
        Positive Reinforcement
        Negative Reinforcement
        Punishment
    Generalization
    Discrimination
    Shaping
    Chaining
    Schedules of Reinforcement
        Variable Ratio
        Fixed Ratio
        Variable Interval
        Fixed Interval

■ SOCIAL LEARNING
    Albert Bandura
    Observational Learning

■ COGNITIVE PSYCHOLOGY AND LEARNING
    E. C. Tolman
    Cognitive Map

B) TEXTBOOK DISCUSSION QUESTIONS

1. *One day little Theodore is extremely startled when he hears the doorbell, and he begins to cry uncontrollably. In the days that follow, stimulus generalization occurs. Describe what might happen during the following days. How would you extinguish his fear?*

Stimulus generalization means that Theodore would cry when hearing SIMILAR bell sounds. The fear might be extinguished by associating something pleasant with the bell sound(s).

2. *Describe a fear that you once had that is pretty much extinguished today. Why or how was the fear extinguished?*

Answers will vary.

3. *Psychologist John Watson once said, "Give me a dozen healthy infants and allow me to control the environment, and I'll make them into anything I want." In other words, he could make them become priests, doctors, or even criminals. Do you agree with him? Explain why or why not.*

This is a good question to discuss in class at the beginning of the unit. Perhaps you can relate their answers to the five approaches discussed in Chapter 1.

4. *According to operant conditioning, people continue to perform certain behaviors mainly because of the reinforcement they receive. This applies even to bad habits. List one of your bad habits. What are several possible reinforcements that you receive for performing the habit? How would you remove or change some of these reinforcements that you receive for performing the habit? How would you remove or change some of these reinforcements and possibly extinguish the bad habit? Here's an example: Habit = biting nails; reinforcement = tastes good; changing reinforcement = apply bitter-tasting polish to nails.*

The nail-biting example in the text describes one way of removing the reinforcement. This removal of the reinforcement would probably work for other habits as well. If a person overeats, this person should not have large quantities of food in his or her house. If a person procrastinates, watching TV instead of doing homework, he or she should remove the TV from the room in which homework is to be completed, or better yet, remove the TV from the house entirely (which may not be entirely realistic). Another method is to DELAY the reinforcement. The person who procrastinates CAN watch TV, but only after a certain amount of homework is completed. Another method is to AVOID situations where or when the bad habit occurs. In this case, you're not really altering the reinforcement, but altering the cues that prompt (not cause) the bad habit. For example, let's say a person swears a lot. In examining the swearing, this person realizes that the swearing occurs only around certain friends. If the motivation to extinguish swearing is high, the person may want to avoid those friends for a while. Another method is to gradually NARROW the cues that prompt the bad habit. For example, if a person wants to quit smoking, he or she could make a list of places (or cues) where smoking occurs. Then the person could rank these places according to the frequency of smoking, 1 being the place where most smoking occurs, the bottom number representing where the least smoking occurs. Each week, the smoker eliminates one of the bottom cues, but continues to smoke during any of the other cues. Eventually, the cues will be narrowed and maybe eliminated.

5. *Imagine a huge gorilla sitting stubbornly in the doorway of his cage, not allowing anyone to close the cage door. How would you use operant conditioning to get him to move? Explain.*

   Ignore the gorilla during undesirable behavior—like sitting in the doorway of his cage. Reward the gorilla for desirable behavior: reward him when he moves—and only when he moves.

6. *If you were a teacher, would you use mainly positive reinforcement, negative reinforcement, or punishment? Explain. Provide specific, practical examples of how you would use the technique you choose.*

   Answers will vary. Perhaps you can discuss which methods are used at your school now.

7. *Many animal trainers use the learning techniques outlined in this chapter to train their animals. If you have a pet, describe in your own words how you have trained the pet to perform certain behaviors. Do you see any similarities between your training techniques and the techniques described in the chapter? For example, did you use shaping and/or chaining? Explain.*

   Answers will vary. This is a good question to discuss in class.

8. *If you wanted someone to become addicted to watching television, which schedule of reinforcement would be most effective? Explain.*

   One of the two VARIABLE schedules would be more likely to promote addiction than the fixed schedules. Point out the addictive nature of gambling (VR) and fishing (VI). A fixed interval schedule would probably be least effective. A person could simply look at his or her watch and sit in front of the TV at the "right" times.

9. *The end of the chapter discusses several techniques for studying. What strategies for studying have been effective for you? Explain.*

   Answers will vary.

C) TEXTBOOK ACTIVITIES

1. Before having students read the chapter, conduct this activity in class. It's a good activity to conduct early to arouse interest in the material.

2. This activity may be difficult for students so it may be a good idea to briefly discuss this one in class. Perhaps you can use yourself as an example and point out the reinforcements that influence you to come to work everyday.

3. Have students who choose to conduct this activity report their conclusions to the class.

4. Again, have students report their findings. Skinner IS fascinating. Perhaps someone can report on the extent that Skinner used behavior modification to raise his children.

5. Definitely conduct this activity in class. It will help to explain shaping and it will help clarify the lengthy directions for the activity.

6. You may want to assign this as a class project and combine everyone's results. Students become excited about large-scale results.

D) IN-CLASS ACTIVITIES / LESSON SUGGESTIONS

1. Just before discussing Pavlov's experiments, bring in a lemon to class. Cut the lemon in half and suck on it, allowing a few drops to drip to the floor. (Is your mouth watering already?) If a lemon is too sour for your tastes, use an orange. The important thing is to get several students to salivate. Once they admit that they're salivating, ask if their responses are learned. The initial reaction will probably be, "No, of course it's not learned. It's natural." There's no question that salivation is natural, but it's NOT natural to salivate after SEEING a lemon. For example, flash a lemon in front of a baby's face, and surely no salivation will occur.

2. Pass out **MASTER 7-2**. It provides students practice in identifying classical conditioning terms.

   Answers to MASTER 7-2
   1. N=Tom's presence; UCS=yell; UCR=blood pressure rising; CS=Tom's presence; CR=blood pressure rising.

   2. N="whoa"; UCS=kick; UCR=go wild; CS="whoa"; CR=go wild.

   3. N=cat's presence; UCS=shock; UCR=fear CS=cat's presence; CR=fear.

   4. N=bell; UCS=medicine; UCR=upset stomach; CS=bell; CR=upset stomach.

3. Here's a fun activity to demonstrate shaping. Have a student volunteer to be a "student rat." Explain that clapping, not food, will be his or her reinforcer. Have the "rat" leave the room. The rest of the class will choose a simple behavior it wants to shape: erasing the board, pulling down the projector screen, and so on. Invite the rat back in. Every time he or she gets close to the desired behavior, the rest of the class will clap. Whenever the rat moves away from the desired behavior, clapping should stop. Students enjoy this activity, and if you repeat the procedure two or three times on other "rats," they become proficient at performing more and more complicated behaviors, such as doing somersaults, standing on your desk, and so on.

4. Print up several homemade "bills" with your name on them: "Jonesdollars," "Smithdollars," and so on. If students collect two (or three or four or whatever) of these bills, they can trade them in for one extra credit point. Hand these bills out throughout the unit as reinforcement for various behaviors, such as asking thoughtful questions, volunteering for an activity, and so on. At the end of the unit, discuss the effectiveness of the bills. Did they improve education or did they interfere? Would it make a difference if the bills were incorporated for a longer period of time? How could the system of awarding the bills be improved?

   You can conduct this activity in several ways. One way is to announce which behaviors will be reinforced and consistently reinforce them. Another way, in another class perhaps, is to include numerous flaws in the procedure. For example, don't announce which behaviors will be rewarded; change the criteria for handing out the bills every twenty minutes or so. Including flaws should demonstrate the need for consistency with any kind of reward system. This can lead to a discussion about the reinforcement "system" at school and in their homes. Are these "systems" consistent?

5. Conduct textbook Activities #1 and #5 in class.

8 Acquiring, Processing & Retaining Information

A. CHAPTER OUTLINE

■ ACQUIRING INFORMATION
    Learning Curves
        Influence of Attention
        Conventional Learning
    Chemical Influences on Learning
    Emotional Factors in Learning
    Transfer of Training
        Positive Transfer
        Negative Transfer

■ INFORMATION PROCESSING
    Schemas
    Organizing Information
    Special Learning Processes
        Elaboration
        Mnemonic Devices
        Principle Learning
        Chunking

■ RETAINING INFORMATION
    Forgetting
        Overlearning
        Forgetting Curve
        Recall
        Recognition
        Interference Theory
    Mechanisms of Memory
    Short- and Long-Term Memory
    Explaining Amnesia
    Unusual Types of Memory
        Eidetic Imagery (Photographic Memory)
        Eyewitness Memory
        Identifying Faces

B) TEXTBOOK DISCUSSION QUESTIONS

1. *Describe the kind of anxiety you experience before a big test. For example, what kinds of physical reactions do you have? What thoughts race through your head? Does this anxiety generally block or help learning? Explain.*

   Answers will vary.

2. *This chapter explains that emotional involvement will usually increase learning. Describe a teacher you have now or have had in the past who "creates emotion" in class. What does the teacher do to "create" the emotion, and what is the effect? Explain.*

   You may suggest that students not use any names.

3. *In a few sentences, describe a time when you've experienced positive transfer and a time when you've experienced negative transfer.*

   Answers will vary.

4. *Which schema would you guess would be more elaborate: (a) deciding to buy and actually buying a pair of shoes or (b) deciding to go to a party? Explain.*

   You may want to discuss this one in class, listing on the board the possible steps involved in both situations. You'll probably find that "deciding to go to a party" will include more steps since it involves an emotional element.

5. *Teachers often use both recall and recognition in their tests. In your opinion, which method more accurately measures how much you actually know? (Be honest.) Explain.*

   Definitely discuss this one in class. Focus not so much on what kinds of tests students prefer, but on what kinds of tests more accurately and thoroughly measure what they know. If students agree that recall tests more accurately measure knowledge, ask if a LENGTHY recognition test (100-200 questions) would compensate for the "superiority" of recall tests.

6. *The chapter explains that patient S's life became a private hell. This may be true, but S's ability might serve him well in certain occupations. Which ones? Explain. What problems would he have even in the occupations that you have listed? Explain.*

   S. would probably do well in occupations where incoming information needs to be processed and organized by the employee at a rapid rate: a worker at the stock exchange; a telephone operator; a secretary in the school's attendance office who must listen to 700 excuses every day. Even in these occupations, S. would still have problems with separating the incoming information and deciding which bits of information were more important than others. If he could simply receive the incoming information and relay it to people who COULD discern the importance of the information, his skills MAY be valuable (although this is still unlikely considering the efficiency of computers).

7. *Imagine someone having the opposite problem of S's-that is, he or she does eliminate all incoming information. Describe a typical experience this person might have.*

This person may read a magazine, put it down, pick up the same magazine seconds later and start to read it without any recollection of reading it moments before.

8. *Research has actually been done to find out which drugs will promote quick, solid consolidation and which drugs will tend to block consolidation. If these drugs were proved to be safe, what proactical applications would each of these drugs have? In other words, when would you want quick consolidation, and when would you want to block consolidation? Explain.*

You might want quick consolidation during important events that you want to be sure to remember later: your marriage vows, your child's first words, and so on. You may want to block consolidation during events that you want to later forget: surgery, a break-up of a relationship, and so on. You can probably think of interesting dilemmas that would result from the availability of such consolidation drugs. For example, would a woman want efficient consolidation during the birth of her child. It may be a glorious event, but does she want to remember EVERYTHING? The pain?

C) TEXTBOOK ACTIVITIES

1. Stress that you're not looking for "correct" schemas. Schema diagrams should demonstrate thought and creativity. Perhaps you can brainstorm and draw a sample schema on the board.

2. Have students hand in their four photographs so you can better understand their reports.

3. This is a simple activity to conduct in class. The students who do not use the mnemonic device should wait outside while you explain the device to the "mnemonic subjects." A week later, surprise both groups of subjects by having them write down as many items on the list as they can remember.

4. The directions for this activity should be self-explanatory. Just insist that the yearbook is old to eliminate the chance of subjects recognizing the faces. Have students "show their work" by requiring students to hand in the photographs.

5. See #4 above. If you require students to conduct more than one activity, you should probably NOT allow them to do both #4 and #5. The problem is that students may conduct only one of these and try to get credit for both.

6. As with Activity #2, collect the photographs used so you can decipher students' reports. Assure them that you will return the photographs without coffee stains on them.

D) IN-CLASS ACTIVITIES / LESSON SUGGESTIONS

1. Here's an activity to use early in the unit to arouse interest in the material and to demonstrate the fallibility of memory. It's a common children's game where the first person whispers a story to a second person who whispers it to a third person, and so on. By the end of the chain, the story has significantly changed. In this case, have four or five students leave the room. Read a story to a volunteer in the room. Then have the students from outside come back one at a time. The volunteer who heard the story will recite it from memory to the first student who will recite it to the second, and so on.

   Here's a possible story that you can use:

   > Jim Large, who weighed 340 pounds, wanted to lose weight. He went to see Dr. Vinnie Rail who prescribed a newly discovered drug. After two weeks of taking the drug, Jim lost fifty pounds. Jim's sister, Jamie, who weighed 190 pounds, found out and visited Dr. Vinnie Rail. After two weeks of taking the drug, she didn't lose a single pound. Instead, her hair began to fall out. Jamie's boyfriend, Jerry, who weighed 120 pounds, became so angry that he charged into Dr. Vinnie Rail's office and started pulling out the doctor's hair. Dr. Vinnie Rail apologized for prescribing the drug and agreed to never prescribe it again. Jim Large, who now weighed 290 pounds, was extremely disappointed that he couldn't use the drug any more. He gained back the fifty pounds he had lost and pulled his own hair out.

   After the activity, which only takes five to ten minutes, discuss how the story changed. What kinds of facts were deleted? Added? Was the doctor's name remembered? It was used four times!

2. Here's a simple activity to demonstrate the necessity of attention for retention. Walk into class one day, get everyone's attention, make a few announcements, then have the students turn their desks around to the back of the room. Prepare a short oral quiz that tests students' recall of objects or signs in the front of the room. Sample questions: "Where is the fire exit sign? What color is it? What does it say on the sign? Is there a flag in the room? Where is it? What color is my shirt?" The purpose of the activity is not to suggest that students SHOULD pay attention to these objects, but the activity should demonstrate the poor performance that results from the lack of attention to these objects.

3. The chapter explains that elaboration helps us store material by using a maximum number of associations. Conduct an activity to see if this applies to short-term memory as well. Have students pair up with one another. Supply one member of each pair a blindfold. Pass out **MASTER 8-4**, face down, to the other member of the pair.

   Half the blindfolded subjects will touch the items listed below. The other blindfolded subjects will touch AND taste the items. Randomly assign which half will follow which procedure. Explain that the items are common, but that they have been assigned different names. The partners who are not blindfolded are simply your experimenters and they will do the following: A) hand the first item to the partner; B) announce the new name of the item and spell it twice; C) listen for your announcement that twenty seconds have elapsed; D) hand over the second item and follow all of the above steps, and so on. These students can follow along with MASTER 8-4 to make sure they are handing over the correct items in the correct order.

   After subjects have touched or touched-and-tasted each item, have them recite the alphabet backwards. Then the experimenters should test each subject's recall, using MASTER 8-4 as a data sheet. The subjects should be presented the items in exactly the same manner as before, but in the different order (**MASTER 8-4** lists the new order). In other words, the "touch" subjects can only touch each item; the other subjects can still touch and taste each item. Be sure that the pairs are separated from each other during this collecting of data so subjects don't overhear one another. Maybe you can eliminate this by sending some pairs just outside the room. Or have each subject softly spell out their responses.

The "taste-and-touch" subjects will theoretically use a greater number of associations to "store" the material than the "touch" group and should have greater recall. Tally and discuss your results.

ITEMS	NEW NAMES
1. peanut	tren
2. popcorn	snop
3. cracker	berc
4. cereal flake	pelm
5. chocolate	corf
6. pretzel	zunt
7. marshmellow	larn
8. sunflower seed	nerp
9. raisin	tilp

4. Conduct textbook Activity #3 in class.

5. You can demonstrate the concept of overlearning by making a list of popular advertising slogans or jingles. It's easy to assemble this list — just brainstorm with a colleague or two. Recite these slogans to your class, but leave out a few key words. The chapter includes a non-advertising example of this: "I pledge allegiance to the _____." See if students can fill in the blanks. It seems that advertisers have mastered the concept of overlearning.

6. The text describes the case of a teacher who staged a fake assault on himself. This is a simple enough activity to do if you can find someone in your school whose face would not be readily recognized for some reason. Have this person charge into class accusing you of hitting his or her car (or think of some other accusation—be creative). To make this confrontation more realistic, maybe you can have the "assailant" knock on your classroom door and call you outside. You can argue for a while outside, out of view from students but not out of earshot. Then you can walk in, pretending to look for something in your desk. The assailant, after waiting outside for a while, can then storm in and verbally attack you. Make sure the assailant doesn't stay in the room too long.

Optional: Have a photograph of the assailant ready, along with the photographs of three or four similar looking people. Spread these photos on your desk and number them. Have the class march by the desk in single file, silently choosing the number of the assailant.

Pass out **MASTER 8-2** to half the class. Pass out **MASTER 8-3** the other half of the class. Have EVERYONE fill out these identical looking sheets, but DON'T point out that the sheets are slightly different. Both include leading questions. On **MASTER 8-2**, questions #3 and #8 are leading; on **MASTER 8-3**, questions #2 and #7 are leading. Point out that the use of the word "assailant" on both sheets may be leading. (Notice that these two Masters provide you with the option of skipping the "photograph" part of the procedure above.)

Afterwards, analyze your results. This activity requires a good deal of effort on your part, but the results are worthwhile. As discussed in the chapter, people learn more efficiently when mildly aroused, when they pay attention. This is a good opportunity to put these concepts into practice. Also, it will bring to life the material on eyewitness memory. If you DO conduct this activity, warn students in your first class not to say anything about the activity to your other classes. A final reminder: conduct this activity BEFORE having students read about eyewitness memory in the text.

9 Intelligence and Creativity

A. CHAPTER OUTLINE

■ UNDERSTANDING INTELLIGENCE
    Defining Intelligence
    Binet Intelligence Test
        Test-Item Construction
        Intelligence Quotient
            Mental Age
            Chronological Age
    Wechsler Intelligence Test
        Verbal Items
        Performance Scale
            Picture Completion
            Object Assembly
        Wechsler Adult Intelligence Scale (WAIS)
    What Is Intelligence?
        Society's Definition
        Is Intelligence Inherited?
    Issues in Intelligence Testing
        Individual Intelligence Tests
        Group Intelligence Tests
        Uses and Limits of I.Q. Scores
        Court Cases
    Brain Size and Intelligence
    Effects of Mental Age

■ CREATIVITY
    Tests of Creativity
    Breaking Set
    Creative Students

■ MENTAL RETARDATION
    Basic Classifications
    Physical Defects
    Environmental Factors
    Methods of Treatment

B) TEXTBOOK DISCUSSION QUESTIONS

1. *Your friend, Jorge, believes that studying intelligence is a waste of time. All it does is allow others to discriminate against people who have low "intelligence." Besides, you can never measure it accurately anyway. Your other friend, Maureen, disagrees. She believes that intelligence testing can single out people of low intelligence and help those people through special programs. With whom do you agree? Why? Explain.*

2. *Imagine that IQ tests made virtually no errors whatsoever. Should grade levels in school then be determined by IQ or by the traditiional chronological method? Explain.*

3. *Imagine you're the boss of a computer programming firm. You're aware of the potential problems with IQ tests (they can make errors), but the courts recently decided that using the tests for hiring was legal. Would you administer IQ tests to potential employees? Why or why not?*

4. *Fascinating research is currently being conducted on ways to increase the efficiency of the brain (despite its already remarkable efficiency). If you were a parent and you could increase the "intelligence" of your future children by taking certain "safe" drugs, would you do it? Why?(This may seem like an incredible possibility today, but it may not seem that incredible by the time you're a grandparent.)*

1-4 Answers to all these questions will vary. Consider discussing the questions in class.

5. *See how creative you can be:Write down "tin can" at the top of a sheet of paper and make a list of 20 original uses for the can. Since creaviviey is being highlighted here, don't feel restricted by the "tin can" suggestion. Choose another everyday object if you like.*

You can adapt this question for classroom use. Make a list of common objects and write each object on a separate index card. Break the class into small groups. Each group will pick a card and think of 20 original uses for the object and later share this list with the rest of the class. Perhaps you can think of a creative "award" for the most creative group!

6. *Do you think that school in general tends to promote or block creativity? List several examples to support your opinion.*

Answers will vary. Students usually enjoy discussing school policies. Discuss these policies, one by one, and ask if the policy promotes or blocks creativity. You might get some interesting and surprising responses. For example, students may complain that the attendance and tardy policies are too strict, but these policies still may promote creativity by forcing students to creatively outwit the system.

7. *In the book Flowers for Algernon, the main character, Charly, is retarded but seemingly happy, in spite of others ridiculing him. He sees the ridicule as friendship. Later, he is the subject of an experiment that increases his intelligence dramatically. His happiness, however, is threatened because now he understands the ridicule. Which extreme would you find preferable: to know and to be usually miserable or to not know and to be happy? Explain.*

Consider discussing this question in class.

8. *If you were tested for "intelligence," on which test do you think you would score highest: Stanford-Binet, Wechsler, or Multiple Intelligences? Explain.*

Answers will vary.

C) TEXTBOOK ACTIVITIES

1. Instead of having students hand in written reports, you might have them summarize and organize their research onto a posterboard and display it in class. If they find any sample intelligence test items, have them include these samples. If not, maybe they can devise their own sample questions.

2. As suggested for previous chapters, demand that students write several of their own interview questions, rather than relying only on the questions listed in the text.

3. Before students hand in this activity, you may want to list an object on the chalkboard, have them write down as many uses as possible for the object, and then analyze which uses are "creative." The main purpose of this is to provide students with practice in analyzing the list. (See In-Class Activity #4 for another way of providing this practice.)

4. Since the purpose of this activity is to "test" the creativity of your students, you should probably avoid discussing a possible system for measuring creativity until after the activity is completed.

5. If possible, have the entire class read FLOWERS FOR ALGERNON. You can refer back to it again when you get to the unit on abnormal psychology. If obtaining a class set of the book is not feasible, consider showing the movie, CHARLY, which is based on the book.

6. Have students report their findings to the class.

D) IN-CLASS ACTIVITIES / LESSON SUGGESTIONS

1. To introduce the unit, write the word "intelligence" on the chalkboard and brainstorm for a definition. This should serve to point out how difficult it is to arrive at a single, concrete definition. Explain that like consciousness, intelligence is a construct (discussed in Chapter 6). Intelligence cannot be seen or touched, but there's plenty of evidence that it exists. Then brainstorm for examples of this evidence.

2. Break the class into small groups and have them write several intelligence test questions. The questions should be designed so that someone their own age group should probably be able to answer them. After each group has written five to ten questions, bring the class together again and discuss the questions. Do the questions seem reliable and valid? Can most students in the class answer the questions? Are the questions culturally biased? If someone from another planet looked at the questions, what conclusions would the alien draw about intelligence on earth? In other words, what kinds of abilities do the questions measure? Academic? Performance?

3. Urge your school psychologist to visit your class to discuss a school's purpose in administering intelligence tests. If this person is willing to come in, have your class prepare beforehand a list of "intelligent" questions for the visit. Also, ask the psychologist to bring in several sample test items, if possible, and to discuss the kinds of questions included on intelligence tests.

4. Use **MASTER 9-2** to conduct in class an adaptation of textbook Activity #3. Photocopy enough copies of the master for about half of your students and cut these sheets in half. You now have enough copies for ALL your students. Pass out the top of the sheets to half of the students in each class and the bottom to the other half. Note that the top of **MASTER 9-2** includes directions that serve to create pressure; the bottom includes directions without pressure. After students complete the sheets, have them exchange papers to "grade" creativity. Have them circle the items that break set. (See textbook Activity #3 for a description of how to do this.)

    Tally the number of items circled for each group and compare your results. Regardless of your results, discuss the types of pressures that MIGHT stifle creativity in real life: schedules, deadlines, strict rules or laws. Are there any circumstances where these pressures might enhance creativity? You might refer back to behaviorism with its emphasis on external, environmental reinforcements. Some argue that these reinforcements do little to enhance creativity, that people perform creative behaviors to satisfy themselves, not to receive external reinforcements. In fact, if too much emphasis is placed on these reinforcements, creativity will most likely decrease.

    A final note: If you have more than one psychology class, consider giving an entire class the "pressure" directions and another class the "nonpressure" directions. This way, YOU can help to create pressure, or vice-versa, through your verbal directions and demeanor.

    The only drawback to this procedure is that you will have to wait until the next day to tally and compare your results.

5. The following is a variation of textbook Discussion Question #5. Bring to class six or seven common, everyday objects: an eraser, a tape dispenser, an old shoe, and so on. (Be creative.) Break the class into small groups and give each group an object. Each group must think of ten original uses for the object. Then the group should pick its favorite use and demonstrate this use to the class. Explain that they can change the object in any way they like: draw on it, punch holes in it, staple it, rip it, and so on.

10 Infancy and Childhood

A. CHAPTER OUTLINE

■ HEREDITY (nature) vs. ENVIRONMENT (nurture)
    Twin Studies

■ DEVELOPMENTAL PATTERNS
    Maturation Processes
    Growth Cycles
    Critical Periods
        Imprinting

■ FAMILY AND CHILD DEVELOPMENT
    Nuclear vs. Extended Family
    Moms Working Outside the Home
    The Father
    Other Influences
    Child Abuse

■ SEQUENCES OF DEVELOPMENT
    Separation Anxiety
    Piaget's Theory of Cognitive Development
        Sensorimotor Stage
        Preoperational Stage
        Concrete Operations Stage
        Formal Operations Stage
    Kohlberg's Theory of Moral Development
        Preconventional Level
        Conventional Level
        Postconventional Level

■ DEVELOPMENT OF LANGUAGE SKILLS
    Processes of Language
    Rules of Language
    Genie (case study)

B) TEXTBOOK DISCUSSION QUESTIONS

1. *Some communities from time to time pass ordinances that ban the sale of toy guns, the implication being that violence is provoked in large part by what we learn in the environment. Do you agree or disagree with this type of ordinance? Why? Explain.*

   You might have students conduct research on communities that have banned toy guns. What reasons do these communities give for banning the toys?

2. *A similar controversy to that described in number 1 involves the portrayal of violence in television programs. In your opinion, do children learn to be violent themselves through these programs? Should the violence be censored in any way? Explain. Note: Many cartoons include vivid violence.*

   Most students will probably insist that violence on TV does not affect children. Just make sure that students support their opinions. Don't allow them to simply state, "Well, violence doesn't affect ME." In order to answer the question, they need to place themselves in the shoes of either young children or parents of young children. Ask: "If you were a parent, would there be any programs on TV that you wouldn't allow your children to watch?"

3. *Describe several aspects of your personality that are clearly influenced mainly by heredity, and describe several aspects that are clearly influenced mainly by the environment.*

   Answers will vary.

4. *Alisha is a mother who works outside the home. She argues that she spends at least two to three hours of quality time with her child every evening. Her friend, Tonya, is a mother who in not employed. She argues that these two to three hours may be quality time for Alisha, but not necessarily for her child; maybe two to three hours of morning time (or afternoon time) would be the time when the child is most open to quality interaction. In other words, maybe the two to three hours in the evening are a "crabby" time for the child, and the child benefits little from the interaction. With whom do you tend to agree? Explain.*

   After students have argued and explained their positions, discuss the general issue of mothers working outside the home. If a couple can afford it, should the mother stay at home with the children? If the mother has a higher paying job than the father, should the father stay at home with the children?

5. *The chapter mentions that all normal children will eventually experience separation anxiety. Not all parents, however, deal with the anxiety in the same way. For example, let's say that a "stranger" picks up the child, and the child begins to cry. Some parents will tend to take the baby away almost immediately to soothe the child; they let the child gradually decide when he or she is ready to approach the stranger. Other parents will let the stranger hold the child, hoping that the child will get used to the stranger, despite the child's continuing anxiety. In your opinion, which approach would promote a stronger and longer-lasting sense of security for the child? Explain.*

   Answers will vary. When discussing this issue in class, present an additional situation: "You want to leave your child at a babysitter's house, and the child is clearly experiencing separation anxiety. Should you slip out without saying goodbye the moment the child becomes preoccupied with something? Or should you make it a point to wave goodbye and reassure the child that you'll be back?" Some students may argue that their answers will vary, depending on the age of the child. This is a valid point, so allow them to insert various ages in the situation.

6. *In your opinion, what level of moral development best describes each of the following situations? (a) A courtroom judge addressing a jury (b) a teacher who rigidly enforces the rules of the school (c) an automobile driver when a cop is around. More than one answer may be possible for each of these situations, but defend your answer. For example, if one of the situations were "a politician addressing a crowd," you might answer preconventional level, arguing that politicians will grant us favors perhaps, but only if we vote for them.*

Accept any answers that are properly supported. The following are possible answers: A) A courtroom judge is probably concerned with protecting people's RIGHTS so he would belong in the postconventional level; OR a courtroom judge might be interested in BRIBERY MONEY, which would put him in the preconventional level. B) A teacher who strictly enforces rules may belong in the conventional level because strict CONFORMITY in school is what SOCIETY expects and wants. C) This driver may be in the preconventional level if he or she is concerned primarily with getting PUNISHED by the cop.

7. *If a person is at the postconventional level of moral development, this same person will probably also be at the formal operations level of cognitive development. Why? In other words, why would a person need to be advanced in his or her cognitive ability in order to be advanced in his or her moral development? Explain.*

Someone in an advanced level of cognitive development will be able to think abstractly, which will help the person understand the long term consequences of his or her actions. This understanding does not guarantee advanced moral development, but without it, advanced moral development is not a likely possibility.

8. *Imagine a very hypothetical situation where a child, for the first two years of his or her life, does little but watch educational programs like "Sesame Street" every hour, every day. Further, imagine that this child experiences almost no interaction with real people. Why would this child develop few, if any, language skills? Explain. (Hint: Refer back to the principles of learning discussed in Chapter 7.)*

The child with little or no interaction will never get reinforced for any responses. Without some reinforcement, the child will remain a passive observer of life. Also, infants certainly need other kinds of stimulation, like touch and movement, to develop properly.

C) TEXTBOOK ACTIVITIES

1. Have students add their own interview questions to the ones already listed in the text.

2. When writing their lists, students will easily identify the physical characteristics that they share with their parents. The mental and behavioral characteristics, however, may be harder to identify, so you may want to spend a few minutes discussing these more elusive characteristics before assigning this activity. Possible MENTAL similarities: "My parents and I are both intelligent; we're highly competitive; we solve problems similarly; we're stubborn." Possible BEHAVIORAL similarities: "My father and I both walk with our feet out; my mother's eyes twitch when she's worried, and so do mine; we both gesture wildly."

3. These kinds of papers are fun to grade and fun to share in class. Urge your students to SHOW rather than TELL when describing their experiences. For example, rather than writing, "I was embarrassed," they can write, "My face turned flush red."

4. Once students note the similarities between Sesame Street and commercials, you might point out that advertisers appeal to the attention span of a child!

5. Obtain several drawings by children and "analyze" them in class. This should serve to point out the need to brainstorm when analyzing the drawings. Also, it should help communicate to students that you're not looking for single, correct interpretations.

6. This activity can lead to an interesting discussion on how parents push their children into athletics, music, and other areas. Most often, this "pushing" is for the children's benefit, but some parents clearly do it to satisfy their own needs, to achieve glory through their children. Perhaps all parents are guilty of this to some extent, and perhaps it is healthy to some extent. Discuss WHEN this pushing becomes detrimental to children.

D) IN-CLASS ACTIVITIES / LESSON SUGGESTIONS

1. Bring into class several several educational toys, demonstrate how they work, and discuss what children can learn from the toys. If bringing in toys is not feasible, bring in a toy catalog and discuss the educational value of the toys in the catalog. If you need assistance in deciding which toys are educational, and so on, simply talk to several teachers at your school who have recently had a baby. (They'll tell you more than you'll ever want to know.) Then break the class into small groups and have each group "design" on paper an educational toy. Afterwards, each group should present its toy to the class, explaining how it works and what it is supposed to teach. If you want these presentations to be more elaborate, allow students a day or two to actually build the toy or a model of the toy.

2. One classroom activity that is nearly always worthwhile is to bring in speakers or visitors from ouside the class. Speakers who volunteer to visit are usually eager to share their expertise and they're usually highly interesting. Even when speakers aren't that compelling, they still serve to break up the day-to-day routine and they provoke questions that wouldn't normally be asked.

   In this case, consider inviting the owner or manager of a day-care center in your area. Have students prepare beforehand a list of questions for the visit.

3. The chapter describes how parents can influence a child's development. One clear way that parents do this is through their methods of discipline. Ask students which methods their parents used. Which methods were effective and which were ineffective?

   Perhaps you can role-play the administration of several of these methods (other than physical punishment). Take five or six index cards and write a misbehavior on each card: coloring a wall with crayons; throwing a ball in the house and breaking a lamp; swearing; and so on. One student can choose a card and another can discipline him or her using one of the methods discussed earlier. Follow this up with a discussion about whether disciplinary methods should vary to fit the "crime."

4. Some of Piaget's "experiments" with children are fascinating. It might be worth conducting research on these experiments and reporting this research to your class. Here are a few examples to demonstrate the preoperational child's inability to understand conservation: A) Draw two rows of five coins on the board. In one row, the five coins should be nearly touching each other; in the other row, the five coins should be spread apart, making that row longer. Which row has more coins? The preoperational child will claim that the longer row has more. B) Draw two big squares on the board; these squares represent two grass fields. In one field draw six identical squares (representing houses) close together. In the other field draw the same six identical squares, but randomly spread these around the. field. Which field has more grass to cut? The preoperational child will claim that the field with the houses close together has more grass to cut since it LOOKS like it has more. C) Draw two tall, narrow glasses filled with an equal amount of water. Draw a short, wide glass next to the two tall glasses. Tell students to imagine emptying the water from one of the tall glasses into the short glass, wherein the water level will appear lower. Which glass has more water? The preoperational child will say that the tall glass has more.

5. Before discussing Kohlberg, present several moral dilemmas and have students decide how they would resolve the dilemmas. Their ultimate resolutions aren't as important as their reasoning behind their resolutions. Afterwards, tactfully categorize some of their responses into Kohlberg's moral levels. Explain that even though a particular response is preconventional, it doesn't necessarily mean that this reflects someone's entire moral character. Another follow-up possibility is to informally measure the frequency of the different types of responses. Did most of their reasoning reflect conventional level morality? Preconventional? Postconventional?

Possible dillemas:
A) Use the attendance-slip dilemma described in the In Focus section of the chapter. You may be surprised at students' responses. B) You see someone shoplifting at a department store. Do you report this person? C) A store clerk makes a mistake when totalling your bill and charges you $20 less for your merchandise. Do you point out the clerk's mistake? D) You are a police officer on duty. You call home and find out that your home is flooding. There are several homes in your patrol area that are also flooding and MAY need your assistance. Do you go home or do you stay on duty and wait for a possible emergency call? (Skim through the newspaper and you should be able to find several REAL dilemmas.)

11 Adolescence

A. CHAPTER OUTLINE

■ DEFINING ADOLESCENCE
    Early Adolescence
    Middle Adolescence
    Late Adolescence

■ PHYSICAL CHANGES
    Sexual Development
        Puberty
        Hormones and Glands
    Physical Growth
    Rates of Maturation
        Early Maturers
        Late Maturers
    Weight
        Anorexia Nervosa

■ PSYCHOLOGICAL CHANGES
    Conformity
        Crowds
        Cliques
        Gangs
    Group Identity
    Individual Identity
        Erik Erikson
        James Marcia
            Identity Foreclosure
            Identity Diffusion
            Moratorium
            Identity Achievement

■ INTELLECTUAL AND MORAL CHANGES
    Jean Piaget
        Formal Operations Stage
    Lawrence Kohlberg
        Postconventional Level
            Social Contracts
            Universal Ethical Principles

■ FAMILY'S INFLUENCE ON ADOLESCENCE

■ ADOLESCENCE IN THE 80'S

B) TEXTBOOK DISCUSSION QUESTIONS

1. *The chapter explains that, in our society, it's difficult to determine when exactly adolescence ends. Do you think you'd rather have the end of adolescence more clearly defined, or do you prefer it loosely defined as it is now? Why?*

   Students' answers may reflect their maturity or their perceptions of their maturity. Those who already consider themselves "adults" will probably not care how the end of adolescence is defined. Those who are confused or frustrated about their identities, which may be positive if they're actively searching for an identity, may welcome a clearly defined ending to adolescence. This may be a generalization and you may not even want to mention it to your students, but maybe it will give YOU some perspective when discussing the question.

2. *If you could be considered, as of this moment, a full-fledged, 100 percent, certified adult, would you want that? Discuss.*

   Answers will vary, depending on students' definitions of "adult." Write ADULT on the chalkboard and allow students a minute or two to freely write down their reactions. Or brainstorm for a definition of adult. According to their reactions or definitions, do adults tend to be one-dimensional: responsible and bossy and narrow-minded? Or can "certified adults" be irresponsible and rebellious and playful, too?

3. *Consider a 15-year-old from a primitive society who becomes an adult after an elaborate ceremony or ritual (rite of passage). Does this 15-year-old, since he or she is considered an adult and since he or she considers himself or herself an adult, experience some of the same conflicts and frustrations that most adolescents in modern society experience? Explain.*

   A 15-year-old has probably been through puberty already, so physical changes would not be a major source of conflict or frustration. Also, the 15-year-old's cognitive and moral development is relatively advanced. The major source of conflict then would be psychological. In our society, adolescents are EXPECTED to explore alternatives and to experience some confusion and frustration when forming identities. A primitive society would NOT expect much confusion or frustration. The question then is this: How important are society's expectations in influencing perceptions and attitudes and maturity? Answers to THIS question will vary.

4. *Most of us at one time or another have been a part of a clique, whether we realized it or not. Why do people form cliques? Explain. Also, do cliques serve any positive or worthwhile functions? Explain.*

   Many people probably "join" cliques to satisfy some kind of security or social need. If these people find it difficult to satisfy these needs in other ways, perhaps cliques then serve a worthwhile function.

5. *Compare the ranges of adolescence (early, middle, late) to Marcia's theory of identity states. When would an adolescent most likely be foreclosed, diffused, in moratorium, and achieved? Explain. (In answering this question, you may be guilty or generalizing, but go ahead.)*

   An adolescent MAY be diffused during early adolescence; at this time, the adolescent may not be ready for serious exploration of values or personal goals. During middle adolescence, an adolescent MAY be in a moratorium state; the adolescent is probably more capable now of struggling with difficult identity issues. During late adolescence, the adolescent could fit into any of the four identity states, the moratorium and foreclosure states being the most likely, the achievement state being the least likely. In other words, MOST adolescents are either struggling over identity issues (moratorium) or have given up and accepted the identity handed to them by others (foreclosed); furthermore, few adolescents have the maturity or experience needed to adequately resolve the struggle (achieved).

6. *Marcia acknowledges that parts of an individual may be foreclosed, another achieved, and so on. For example, an individual may make a firm and personally meaningful commitment to career and be achieved in this area, but this same individual may wander and be diffused in matters of religion, for example. Pick three of the four identity states and explain how you might fit into each category at this stage in your life.*

Answers will vary.

7. *As mentioned in the chapter, surveys show that teenagers and adults agree on important issues: education, work, politics, drugs. If you and your parents were surveyed on these four areas, what would the results be? Would the agreement be high? Explain.*

Consider discussing this one in class.

8. *No matter how well we get along with our parents as adolescents, there comes a point when we need to break away and begin to assert our own independence. There are several ways in which we do this, some of them deliberate and intentional and some of them not so intentional. For example, someone might join an activity at school for the enjoyment of it, which also causes this person to spend less time at home; as a result (but without really trying for this result), this person probably becomes more independent. Describe several ways, intentional or not intentional, that you use or have used to break away from your parents. Also, briefly describe your parents' past or present reactions to these ways.*

Most students will probably EXPLAIN how they break away from parents, which is fine. But consider telling students to pick ONE vivid expérience that served to help break them away from their parents and to DESCRIBE that experience in detail. These are good papers to read aloud.

9. *Read through the rules of communication listed at the end of the chapter. Which one seems to be the hardest one for you to follow? Offer examples.*

Answers will vary.

C) TEXTBOOK ACTIVITIES

1. This activity seems simple enough, but students may need assistance. Spend a few minutes in class brainstorming for ideas. For example, our society highly values the automobile. Therefore, you can propose that a young person needs to go through a rite of passage to attain a driver's license. In other words, only an adult should be able to drive a car. In this case, the rite of passage would dictate perhaps that the young person needs to prove that he or she can take apart a carburetor and put it back together again!

2. After students complete this activity, conduct a follow-up discussion. Students usually enjoy discussing the group "structures" at their school. You may notice that students find it easy to recognize clique behavior in others, but rarely admit that they themselves belong to any cliques!

3. Students should have no difficulty finding information on these topics.

4. Parents enjoy this kind of involvement.

5. If given a choice of activities to complete, not many students will choose this one. To make this activity seem more appealing, provide students with a general overview of Erikson's theory and "sell" the theory.

6. Even unmotivated students often do a good job with this activity. Bring in a few songs from your own music collection and analyze the lyrics in class. See #4 in Section D below for ideas.

7. This activity is a pleasure to grade and it allows you to become better acquainted with your students. Assure students that the reports will remain confidential, that they will not be read aloud or discussed in class.

D) IN-CLASS ACTIVITIES / LESSON SUGGESTIONS

1. This chapter CAN be one of students' favorites because it deals with THEM! Here are a couple of things you can do to help ensure the chapter's appeal. A) Discuss the word "adolescence." For many students, the word denotes teeny-bopper or something equally demeaning. You need to recognize the negative connotations of the word and encourage students to put aside these connotations. Explain that if they would rather not label themselves adolescents, that it's okay. However, for the sake of discussion, YOU may refer to them as adolescents from time to time, and they should not be offended. B) Allow plenty of time for students to provide personal examples and reactions to the material in the chapter.

    Possible questions to use throughout discussion of the chapter:
    * When does adolescence end?
    * What are some biological changes that you experienced during early adolescence?
      Do you remember any of your "growth spurts" and your reactions to them? (Biological changes can still be a sensitive issue for some students, but if handled tactfully, it can be fun and worthwhile. For example, not many girls will volunteer to discuss their menstrual periods, but YOU might introduce the topic and ask a less threatening question like, "If you were a mother, would you be sure to warn your 8- or 9-year-old daughter about her menstrual period? Why is this important? What age should the daughter be before discussing this?")
    * How did your classmates in junior high react to early maturers? Late maturers?
    * Do you know anyone with a weight problem? What is the problem? How does the person deal with the problem? (No names, please.)
    * What kinds of cliques exist at school? (See if any students in your class have recently transferred to your school and get their "objective" reactions to the cliques at your school.)
    * Did you ever become frustrated .because "you think too much"? (This would be related to the new cognitive skills that adolescents acquire.)
    * Are most of your arguments with your parents over major issues or over minor conflicts like curfew, and so on?
    * How do you break away from your parents?
    * Why do adults sometimes have a difficult time understanding adolescents?
    * Are adults in your world (parents, teachers, counselors) pushing you to grow up quickly or to take your time growing up?
    * Are your parents overprotective?
    * How many times has your family moved? How does this affect growing up?

2. Conduct textbook Activity #1 in class. Brainstorm for ideas with the entire class for a few minutes, just so students understand the activity. Then break the class into small groups, each group creating a rite of passage. After ten minutes or so, have each group report their plan to the rest of the class.

3. If you conduct In-Class Activity #2 above, you might want to use this as a follow-up. Read textbook Discussion Question #3 and allow students about ten minutes in class to respond to the question, using the rite of passage they created in their small groups.

4. Conduct textbook Activity #6 in class. Sift through your own music collection and find six or seven songs that correspond well to Marcia's identity states and analyze the lyrics in class. This should serve to summarize the main points of Marcia's theory and to clarify the particulars. For example, a singer may cry out about the pain and struggle that he or she is experiencing, which would signify a crisis, but if the singer turns his or her back on the crisis and stops searching for values, beliefs, and so on, the "crisis" becomes meaningless. If this same singer makes no commitment, he or she would be classified as identity diffused (and not moratorium as appearances might

imply); if a commitment IS made, then the singer would be identity foreclosed (and not identity achieved as appearances might imply).

Here are possible songs you can use:

"Father and Son"	Cat Stevens	The son is moratorium. The father is trying to foreclose the son.
"The Pretender"	Jackson Browne	The singer makes a safe commitment after turning his back on a crisis: identity foreclosed.
"I am a Rock"	Simon & Garfunkel	The singer wants no commitment and no crisis: identity diffused.
"Honky Cat"	Elton John	The singer seems to be identity achieved.
"She's Leaving Home"	The Beatles	The daughter is moratorium. The parents want to foreclose her.

5. An alternative to In-Class Activity #4 is to bring in several poems and relate the poems to Marcia's identity states.

6. One of the most worthwhile activties to conduct during this unit is to invite parents to class to discuss their own adolescence. Sell the idea of a parent visit to your students and have several students promise to invite their parents. The next day or so, find out how many parents will participate. If you can get at least five or six parents to visit, the discussion should be worthwhile. If you can't get enough parents for one reason or another, you might try sending several students (who have volunteered) to a phone to call their parents during class. Many times, students simply forget to ask, and this should eliminate that problem.

The main purpose of the visit is to compare and contrast adolescence today with adolescence 15 or 20 years ago. The parents who visit are not experts, but they can provide personal observations that are often more insightful than many written sources.

Possible discussion questions for parents:
- How has the attitude toward WORK changed in the past 20 years or so ? What were YOUR parents' attitudes toward work? Did males and females have different career expectations when you were younger?
- How have neighborhoods changed in the last 20 years or so? Have these changes had any effect on the family?
- Were you encouraged to grow up quickly when you were young, or were you told to take your time? Were you encouraged to go to college?

- Did adults 20 years ago command more automatic respect from adolescents than adults do today? If yes, why do you think this has changed?
- Do you feel that today's adolescents have more choices to make than the adolescents of 20 years ago?
- Did adolescents 20 years ago experience more hardships than today's adolescents? Did you really have to walk 20 miles to school?

Try to save the last five minutes of class for a role-playing exercise. Get two parents to play teenagers and get two students to play parents. Paint a scenario that involves conflict. For example, the two "teenagers" have arrived home at 3 AM and the "parents" are worried and angry!

12 Adulthood and Aging

A. CHAPTER OUTLINE

■ FINDING ADULTHOOD

■ LATE ADULTHOOD / EARLY ADULTHOOD
   Mid 20's
   30-35 Years

■ MIDLIFE TRANSITION 40-45

■ MIDDLE ADULTHOOD 45-60
   Empty Nest Period
   Menopause
   Mellow 50's

■ LATE ADULTHOOD: OVER 60 (Gerontology)

■ AGING PROCESS
   Cellular Time Clocks
   Mental Ability of the Aged
         Health and Mental Ability
         Intelligence and Aging
         Senility
               Cerebral Arteriosclerosis
               Alzheimer's Disease

■ CONCERNS OF THE AGED
   Retirement
   Isolation and Bereavement
   Attitudes Toward Old Age
   Institutionalization

■ THANATOLOGY
   Hiding From Death
   Issues Regarding Death
   Stages of Dying
   Help for the Dying
         Hospices

B) TEXTBOOK DISCUSSION QUESTIONS

1. *As noted in the chapter, society still views "man's work" as more significant than woman's. If you're a male, would it bother you if your wife's career was more "significant" than yours and if she made much more money than you? Why or why not? Be honest. If you're a female, would it bother you if you made more money than your husband? Why or why not?*

   Answers will vary—and so will the honesty of the answers.

2. *When you hear about research on manipulation of genes to prolong the life span, do you tend to become excited about the prospect, or do you think the life span is something that really shouldn't be toyed with and manipulated by science? Argue for one of these points of view.*

   Answers will vary. Consider having two or more students debate the issue in class for a few minutes and follow this up with a general discussion.

3. *The chapter explains that the number of people over 65 has increased dramatically and will probably continue to increase. Let's assume that many of these people choose not to retire; consequently, the unemployment rate among young people rises sharply. Should the older people be forced to retire? Why or why not? Explain.*

   Answers will vary. Students may have difficulty viewing the situation from the point of view of someone other than a young person who will soon need a job. Remind them that one day THEY may be the ones forced to retire.

4. *If you were about 75 years old and were unable to live independently, do you think you'd prefer to live in a well-run nursing home so you could associate with others your age, or do you think you'd rather live with your own children (assuming they welcome you!)? Explain.*

   Again, students may have difficulty putting themselves in the shoes of an old person. At this point in their lives, they are probably looking forward to being on their own, to leaving their parents. Emphasize the need to answer the question from an older person's point of view.

5. *The chapter describes several ways in which or society tends to ignore the reality or death. For example, even sympathy cards avoid mentioning words like "death" and "dying." What are some other ways in which we ignore it? Explain. Consider language, hospital procedures, and funeral rituals.*

   Here are some other examples of how we ignore death. The words "death" and "dying" often become: passed away; deceased; put to sleep (as with animals); no longer with us; united with God. Dead people are often referred to as the "beloved." These examples may be trivial, but they're representative of a more general evasion of the existence of death. Point out, however, that oftentimes this evasion serves a worthwhile function. For example, when a person dies, the wake, the funeral, and the burial, though they may seem to encourage an evasion of death at times, allow the family and friends of the dead person time to grieve, time to accept the reality of the death.

6. *If you found out that you had only a year to live, would you be likely to continue to live life as usual, or would you drastically alter your life-style? Explain. If you were to change your life drastically, what would you do differently? Be specific.*

This is a good topic to use as an in-class journal entry.

7. *Imagine that you're a parent and your 18-year-old son announces that he wants to marry the 16-year-old girlfriend he has been dating for the past two years. Would you try to talk him out of it? Why or why not? Would your answer be different if the situation were somewhat reversed, and your 18-year-old daughter announced that she wanted to marry her 18-year-old boyfriend? Explain.*

This is a good situation to role-play in class.

C) TEXTBOOK ACTIVITIES

1. This activity should be of high interest to students since it offers insights into their near futures. Have students who complete this acitvity share these insights with the rest of the class.

2. Consider conducting this activity in class over the course of a week, allowing about ten minutes per journal entry. Afterwards, try to get volunteers to read aloud one of their favorite entries.

3. Students clearly have fun conducting this experiment. Remind them, however, that they need to remain objective and scientific when collecting data. For example, they need to drop the contents of the bag in an identical manner for every subject. You may even want to bring a shopping bag to class and have a student or two demonstrate HOW they will drop the contents in the bag.

   Tell students to consider videotaping the experiment. These tapes are a pleasure to watch in class; and they're enlightening!

4. Students will do a great job with this one! Encourage them to be creative and humorous.

5. Pick one or two of the better dialogues and have students play them out in class.

6-7. Consider having students present their information to the class. High school students probably don't know a great deal about these topics and oral presentations should provide a good opportunity to not only hear about these topics, but to ask questions.

D) IN-CLASS ACTIVITIES / LESSON SUGGESTIONS

1. A good way to introduce the chapter is to have students draw a time line on a sheet of paper, the beginning of the line representing their births, the end representing their deaths. Have them place an "x" somewhere near the beginning of the line to mark the present. Above this "x" they should write their ages; below the "x" they should write "the present." Have them fill out the rest of the time line in a similar way, marking significant ages and events of the past and marking their predictions about the future. How old will they be when they get married, have children, and so on? The purpose of the activity is to force students to think more realistically about their futures. The more often and effectively you can accomplish this, the more meaningful will be the material in the chapter. Another way of forcing students to think about their futures is to have them complete textbook Activity #2. See Section C above for ideas.

2. Introduce the section on Late Adulthood by writing the word "old" on the board. Go around the room and have each person name one thing that comes to mind when hearing the word "old." You'll get responses like "frail, senile, lonely, wrinkled," and so on. Write their responses on the board and review each one by placing an M next to each response that is MYTH, and an R next to each response that is REALITY. (Have the class discuss and decide which responses are myth and which are reality.) You'll probably notice a pattern. Most of the reality-responses will be associated with inevitable physical decline; most of the myth-responses will be associated with intellectual decline or emotional deficiencies (lonely, withdrawn, and so on). This simple activity should make students more aware of their own myths surrounding old age; and it should urge them to question those myths.

3. In Chapter 11 we suggested that you invite parents to class to discuss adolescence. This may not be as feasible, but you might try to invite grandparents to class to discuss some of the issues presented in the chapter.

4. One of the traditional poet's common themes is about death. Have each student find a "death" poem and present it to the class, explaining the poet's message. Students may be surprised to find that these messages are not necessarily morbid or depressing (which is an idea you may want to sell to your students beforehand). In fact, good poetry, even when the topic is death, will usually be profound and uplifting in some way.

   Finding these poems should be relatively easy. Tell students to skim through the table of contents or index of a poetry anthology and look for a reference to death. Or just have them ask their English teachers for suggestions.

5. Bring construction paper and several boxes of crayons to class and allow students about ten minutes to "draw death." They will probably have a variety of questions, but try not to give them any other suggestions. Afterwards, have students display their drawings by taping them to the front of their desks. Then tell them to get in a circle and have them briefly explain their drawings. Finally, discuss their interpretations of death. Are they morbid, uplifting, depressing? Are their renditions of death influenced by Hollywood or books or fairy tales or religion?

6. If you try the "death activities" above, you need to be sensitive to the reactions of students. If most students are extrememly defensive about drawing death, and so on, you probably shouldn't dwell on the subject. If most students seem receptive to discussing death—and most of them will be if YOU are "excited" about it—here's another possible activity. Allow them about ten or fifteen minutes in class to write their obituaries. If they had died yesterday (and they should date these as yesterday rather than today or tomorrow, which may seem more ominous), how would they be remembered today? Emphasize that the focus here is not really on their deaths, but on their lives

They can list their accomplishments, their positive characteristics, their relationships, and so on. A possible follow-up to this activity is to have them write their obituaries as if they had died at the age of eighty. What WILL be their accomplishments, and so on?

7. You may want to spend a few minutes discussing how you would explain death to a six- or seven-year-old child. What are some things you would NOT do? For example, why wouldn't you say that the dead person is sleeping or on vacation? What are some things that you would do? Consider reading FREDDIE THE LEAF, by Leo Buscaglia, in class. Ask if the book would be appropriate for explaining death. Can they think of any other stories that appropriately explain death?

8. If you like the idea of panel presentations (where four or five students present reports to the class), this chapter lends itself well to this method since there are so many interesting related issues that students can explore. Here is a list of possible topics:

- Mercy Killing
- Life Support Machines
- Near Death Experiences
- Living Wills
- Wills
- Abortion
- Suicide
- Funeral Homes
- Hospices
- Alzheimer's Disease
- Institutionalization

A WARNING:

Panel presentations CAN become boring. This usually occurs when the panel lectures to the class without encouraging any involvement. To avoid this, tell students that their "formal" reports need not be lengthy. Rather, they should focus on discussion questions that involve the class. You may even demand that each panel write 20 or 30 discussion questions, warning them that a major portion of their grades will be based on the thoughtfulness of the questions. If you're worried that students will not conduct enough research with this emphasis on discussion, simply require them to hand in a written report before the presentations. Even though you may want to suggest a time limit for the presentations, you probably don't want to be so strict that you cut off a lively discussion just because "time is up."

13 Gender Differences

A. CHAPTER OUTLINE

- **GENDER MYTHS**

- **THE ROLE OF HORMONES**
    - Androgen
    - Estrogen

- **MALE / FEMALE DIFFERENCES**
    - Child Bearing
    - Activity and Aggression

- **INTELLIGENCE**
    - Spatial Skills
    - Mathematical Ability
    - Environmental Influences

- **SOCIAL SKILLS**
    - Self-Confidence
    - Drive for Success
    - Maternal Instincts

- **HORMONAL CYCLES**
    - Menstrual Cycles
    - Premenstrual Syndrome

- **MARRIAGE**

- **GENDER ROLE BEHAVIOR**
    - Identification
    - Psychologically Generated Gender Roles
        - Mixing Gender Roles
        - Androgyny

B) TEXTBOOK DISCUSSION QUESTIONS

1. *If you were a parent, would you ever consider buying your daughter a toy machine gun or toy soldiers? Why or why not?*

2. *If you were a parent, would you ever consider buying your son a doll or a toy kitchen set? Why or why not?*

1-2. Consider reading students' responses aloud in class. Are there any patterns that develop? Is one sex more flexible or more open-minded than the other? If so, in what way does society promote this flexibility (or inflexibility)?

3. *If you took a survey, you'd probably find that despite a leveling of gender role differences today, males still are primarily responsible for asking girls out for a first date. In your opinion, why do a majority of females usually refrain from initiating dates? Explain.*

    After students answer this question, ask the males in class why THEY oftentimes refrain from asking girls for dates. Compare and contrast these responses to the responses to the discussion question. You'll probably find some striking similarities. For example, both males and females will certainly admit their fears of rejection. The main difference then will be society's expectations of what each sex should do.

4. *Many people advocate passage of an Equal Rights Amendment (ERA) that would ban sex discrimination. Others argue that laws already exist to stop this discrimination. Furthermore, passage of the ERA would mean that women could be drafted in the event of a war. Assuming that these critics are right about women being drafted, should the ERA still be passed? Why or why not?*

    Answers will vary. Consider debating the issue in class.

5. *All of us are androgynous to some extent. Describe several of your own characteristics that reveal your androgyny. In other words, describe some of your "masculine" traits and some of your "feminine" traits.*

    Compare and contrast boys' responses to the question to girls' responses. Is one sex more willing to admit its androgyny?

6. *This part of the question is for the males: Describe the advantages of being a female. This part is for the females: Describe the advantages of being a male.*

    These responses can be hilarious. Consider requiring students to write at least a page on this question, and then read these papers aloud in class.

C) TEXTBOOK ACTIVITIES

1-2. Students should have fun with these activities. The chances are slim, but if you have a student named "Roanoke" in your school, make up a different name.

3. Since students won't be able to rip out the old ads from magazines in the library (and warn them not to) have them briefly describe the ads that they use. If you think it's necessary, you may even have them include a rough sketch of some of the more important ads that they use.

4. Some students do an excellent job with this activity. Again, warn them not to rip out the ads from the magazines in the library.

5. To prepare students for this activity, discuss the questions listed in Psychology in Your Life at the end of the chapter. The nature of the questions should provoke lively responses. As you listen to these responses, run to the chalkboard every once in a while to write down several of them. Afterwards, analyze the responses on the board: Are they sexist and traditional?

   If you have time, you might also want to brainstorm for interview questions needed for the activity.

6. Have students add their own questions to the ones already listed in the text.

7. Warn students that magazines can become highly technical in their coverage. Encourage them to choose magazines that are readable.

D) IN-CLASS ACTIVITIES / LESSON SUGGESTIONS

1. If your school is not coeducational, some of the following activities will obviously not apply. You may be able to adapt some of them into assignments.

   Photocopy **MASTER 13-2**, cut it in half, and hand the top portion to half of your students and the bottom portion to the other half. Note that the top portion includes the name Jim, whereas the bottom portion uses the name Jane. (Do NOT make students aware of this.) Have students complete the directions on the master. The purpose of the activity is to see if students will write more positive endings to the JIM story than to the JANE story.

   Collect students' responses and read them aloud in class. After each one, decide if the ending is basically positive, negative, or neutral, and keep a tally on the chalkboard. If the Jim-stories are much more positive than the Jane-stories, you might conclude that traditional gender role expectations still influence many of your students. If so, discuss why. Do their parents still promote this? Does society? What if the situation were altered a bit, and Jim and Jane were just graduating from college with degrees in art or education? Would their responses be different? If there are not any significant differences between the two stories, discuss why. Do their parents or society promote THIS? In what ways?

2. As a follow-up to In-Class Activity #1, try to get a current grade school reader and read several of the short stories to your class. Do these readers promote traditional gender role behavior? If possible, also obtain a grade school reader used ten or twenty years ago and compare and contrast this one with the current reader. If you can't obtain any readers, try comparing and contrasting ANY old and new children's books.

3. It might be fun to create some friendly competition between the males and females in your class. Propose the hypothesis that males have greater spatial skills than females, and that females have better verbal skills than males. Use **MASTER 13-3** and **13-4** to test this hypothesis. Pass out **MASTER 13-3** face down, have everyone begin solving the puzzles at the same time, and time them. As students finish, they can raise their hands, and you can give them their times. (Or students can break into pairs and partners can time each other.) Follow the same procedure for **MASTER 13-4**, but instead of timing them individually, simply give them all a one-minute time limit. Tally the results, comparing which sex scored higher and which sex finished the spatial skills sheet more quickly. Try to draw several conclusions from your results; refer to the material in the text for ideas.

Answers to MASTER 13-3:		Answers to MASTER 13-4:	
1.	b	1.	c
2.	d	2.	b
3.	two	3.	a
4.	one	4.	d
5.	two	5.	a
		6.	d
		7.	b
		8.	a
		9.	c
		10.	a

4. Now that the two sexes have battled, continue the battle with one of two new hypotheses. If you are a man, propose that "Males are more athletic than females"; if you are a woman, propose the opposite. "More athletic" will be defined as the ability to throw a ball into a bucket from increasing distances. All you need for this activity is one ball and one "bucket"; you can use the trash can as the bucket. Mark a starting line on the floor and mark six spots where you will place the bucket; the first spot should be one foot away from the starting line and will be worth one point; the second spot should be two feet away and will be worth two points, and so on. Use as many subjects as you like.

    The real purpose of this activity is to observe how males and females compete against one another. Is the "drive for success," in this case, similar? Who treats the game more seriously? Who is more vocal? Who jokes around more? WHY is one sex more vocal or jocular; is this sex using jokes to cover up real feelings about the game?

    You probably don't want to go too far with these conclusions—after all, it IS only a game—but ask students to be honest with their answers to the above questions, and you should be able to arrive at some interesting insights. Since YOU are the only one aware of the true purpose of the game, pay close attention during the game; you might even want to sit in the back of the room, pretending to keep score, but actually writing down your observations.

5. If your class enjoys role-playing, you can have fun assigning females roles to males and male roles to females. Some of this role playing will become exaggerated and downright silly, but it can lead to an interesting discussion of each gender's perception of the other. After each situation is played out, perhaps you can list on the board the perceptions portrayed by the role-players. Discuss why these perceptions exist and whether they're accurate.

    Possible role-playing situations:
    a) A "boy" is asking a "girl" for a first date.
    b) Two "girls" are talking about another girl whom they do not like.
    c) Two "boys" are talking about another boy whom they do not like.
    d) A "girl" is breaking off a relationship with a "boy."
    e) A "boy" is breaking off a relationship with a "girl."
    f) A "girl" calls home pleading to her "mom" that she wants to stay out later.
    g) A "boy" pleads with his "dad" to use the car.

    You might want to print these situations onto index cards and have students pick a card after they volunteer.

14 Theories of Personality

A. CHAPTER OUTLINE

- **DIFFICULTIES IN DEALING WITH PERSONALITY**
  - Usefulness of Theories
  - Defining Personality
- **PSYCHOANALYSIS**
  - Sigmund Freud
  - The Unconscious
    - Free Association
    - Repression
- **THE LIBIDO**
- **FREUD'S MAP OF THE MIND**
  - Id
  - Superego
  - Ego
- **FREUD'S STAGES OF DEVELOPMENT**
  - Oral Stage
  - Anal Stage
  - Phallic Stage
  - Latency Stage
  - Genital Stage
- **ASSESSMENT OF FREUD**
- **CARL JUNG**
  - Collective Unconscious
  - Persona
- **ASSESSMENT OF JUNG**
- **SOCIAL PSYCHOANALYTIC THEORIES** (neo-Freudians)
  - Karen Horney
  - Alfred Adler
  - Erik Erikson
  - Assessment of Neo-Freudians
- **BEHAVIORISM**
  - B.F. Skinner
    - Reinforcement
  - Albert Bandura
    - Modeling
  - Assessment of Behaviorism
- **HUMANISTIC THEORIES** (Humanism)
  - Carl Rogers
    - Ideal Self
    - Fully Functioning Individual
  - Abraham Maslow
    - Self-Actualized
  - Assessment of Humanism
- **EXAMINING PERSONALITY TRAITS**
  - Major Permanent Traits
  - Effects of the Environment

B) TEXTBOOK DISCUSSION QUESTIONS

1. *There was a time when it was very fashionable to be psychoanalyzed. Whey do you suppose it was popular? Also, do you think you would ever want to be psychoanalyzed? Why or why not?*

   Psychoanalysis became popular, in part, because of its initial emphasis on sex. Since sex was not openly discussed in Freud's time, people were eager to adopt an "appropriate" mode for discussing it: psychoanalysis.

   Answers to the second part of the question will vary. Mention that their analyses need not be conducted by a Freudian, who would emphasize sexual motivation, but by a neo-Freudian who would emphasize social forces.

2. *Sharon suffers from a severe bout of depression. How would Horney's explanation of her depression differ from Adler's?*

   Horney would probably argue that Sharon is not receiving enough love. Adler would insist that Sharon does not feel important or worthwhile.

3. *Freud was probably correct to some extent in saying that much of our personality remains the same as we grow. Erikson was also probably correct to some extent in saying that much of our personality does change. Think back on your junior high school years. Describe aspects of your personality that have changed and aspects that have remained essentially the same.*

   Answers will vary.

4. *If you were suffering from depression over the breakup of a relationship and you decided you wanted to see a therapist, would you prefer to talk with a behaviorist or with a humanist? Why?*

   Students will have a better grip on this question after they read the chapter on treatments and therapies. For now, be sure they support their answers with material from the chapter. A behaviorist would analyze depression in terms of behavior: Is the person sleeping less, eating less, crying more? The behaviorist would then try to pinpoint the specific conditions that cause or are associated with these behaviors. A humanist, on the other hand, would view the depression in a more holistic manner: How is the person feeling about life, about the depression. Ultimately, according to the humanist, the person has the inner strength to heal himself or herself; the humanist would simply help the person realize this strength.

5. *As noted in the chapter, implementing humanism in the classroom in the 1960's turned out to be a disaster. Despite this, some people might argue that there's nothing wrong with applying humanistic ideas in the classroom, as long as certain guidelines are set. Propose a humanistic change you'd like to see adopted at your school. Make the proposal practical and somewhat detailed. (A "humanistic" change would be one that would encourage students to handle their own fates.)*

   Students enjoy criticizing school policies, but rarely offer practical alternatives. This is their chance to do the latter. Consider discussing this question in class. Here are some possible humanistic changes that students may mention:

1) Students should be given more long-range due dates for assignments. It will be up to students to budget their time. In college, most assignments are handled in this way. (Can high school students handle this? Probably not. Even a behaviorist would admit that changing one small aspect of the environment may not be enough to alter behavior.)

2) Students should be allowed to roam the halls whenever they like. The ones who disturb classes should be put in study halls.

3) Students should be able to choose their own classes and teachers and schedules. (This suggestion should provoke a lively discussion.)

6. *If you could magically change one aspect of your personality—right now—would you choose to change something? If so, what would you change and why? If not, why not? Also, what is one aspect of your personality that you would never change? Explain.*

You should get some interesting responses to this question. Consider discussing it in class. If you do, you MAY be able to categorize some of their answers as psychoanalytical, behavioral, or humanistic. The purpose of this categorization is not to pigeonhole their responses or personalities, but to elucidate the three theories.

7. *The chapter explains that three personality traits seem to be inherited: friendliness, trying new things, and anxiety. Does this conclusion accurately describe you own life? Why or why not? Describe in detail several of your traits and compare these traits with other members of your family.*

Answers will vary.

8. *Out of all the theories presented in the chapter, which one seems best suited to understanding someone with a severe mental disorder, and which one is best suited to understanding someone who is relatively healthy? Explain.*

The most likely responses will be that Freud's theory best explains mental disorders—Freud treated hysterical patients—and that humanism best explains healthy behavior since it emphasizes self-actualization.

C) TEXTBOOK ACTIVITIES

1. The directions for this activity should be self-explanatory. Also, the activity is simple to adapt to classroom use. Warn students that if subjects are not supplying reasons for their choices, maybe they (your students) can read the statements aloud to give subjects more cues. Or maybe students can write 5 short paragraphs rather than single sentences. In other words, it is up to your students to prompt reasons for choices from subjects.

2. Students should have no difficulty finding information on either of these topics.

3. Since the directions for this activity are so lengthy, you might want to spend a few minutes in class fielding questions. Also, have students make a list of clothes (and hairstyles) that a "traditional" and a "radical" model would wear. If you can pare down this list and convince all traditional models and all radical models to dress almost identically, perhaps you can tally everyone's results and draw overall conclusions with some degree of validity. Even if you do not plan on combining everyone's results, it's probably a good idea to devise a consistent and somewhat objective definition of traditional and radical for your area; it will communicate to students the need to be consistent when collecting data.

4. See #3 above. In this case, all you'll need to determine is what constitutes "young" and "old."

5. Again, since the directions are so lengthy, spend a few minutes in class fielding questions. Encourage students to be sincere in their descriptions; the more sincere they are, the more meaningful the activity will be. Consider allowing students to choose their own five categories for the activity; this freedom of choice may make the activity more appealing. Finally, assure students that their descriptions will not be read aloud in class; this may promote more openness on their part.

6. Discuss the results of this activity in class. It can lead to an interesting discussion on dating.

D) IN-CLASS ACTIVITIES / LESSON SUGGESTIONS

1. When students learn about Freud's theory, they sometimes dismiss it as ancient and, consequently, never really understand it. To help students appreciate Freud's ideas, you might want to provide them with a vivid picture of Freud's background; if students can view Freud as a man and not just as the owner of a theory, they may become more interested in his ideas. There are a couple of ways to do this. The first is easy: Just bring in two or three library books that include photographs of Freud and his family and show them to your students. If the books include synopses of his case studies, you may want to briefly recount several of these. The other method of highlighting Freud is more ambitious. Get a pair of costume glasses and a cigar and BECOME Freud for 20 or 25 minutes. Announce one day that you invited a guest speaker to class, leave, then return as Freud: "My name is Sigmund Freud. I was born in 1856, and-unfortunately—I died in 1939..." This "role-playing" requires a good deal of preparation, but most students appreciate the extra effort.

2. Once students understand Freud's ideas, the next step is to demonstrate how these ideas somehow relate to today's world. For example, Freud certainly did not discover the unconscious, but he was the first to "scientifically" study it. As a result of his extensive efforts, we now take for granted the idea of the unconscious (though many down-play its importance).

   To demonstrate the possible existence of this unconscious, conduct an adaptation of textbook Activity #1. Break the class into groups of three and have each group choose one theme—for example, "The time I was in the hospital," or "My most embarrassing moment," and so on. Two of the members of each group will recount real experiences on the group's theme; the third member will tell a complete lie. Each story should last about a minute.

   Allow them very little time to prepare (4-5 minutes). Then have each group come to the front of the room to present its stories. The point is that the liar cannot successfully lie without revealing him or herself; the liar will unconsciously give him- or herself away. Test how true this is by having the class vote on the liar after each group presentation.

   After two or three presentations, you might want to send the fourth group out of the room while the class discusses a "system" of detecting the liar. For example, you can count the number of pauses and the number of fillers, like "you know"; you can note eye movements, abrupt gestures, and so on. Or you can devise this system after all groups are done; send the "best" three liars out of the room to think of new stories while the class devises its system, and then test the system on the liars.

3. Another way that the unconscious theoretically reveals itself is through body language and handwriting. Though many perceive these topics as "pop" psychology, students are highly interested in them. Consider conducting research on these topics and presenting this research to your class. If you'd rather not prepare this information, offer extra-credit to several students who are particularly interested in the topics and who will conduct the research.

Even without research you can demonstrate different kinds of body language. For example, fold your arms or sit back with your hands behind your head or cross your legs, and brainstorm what these behaviors might mean. Another possibility is to play a simple body language game. Have five students leave the room; assign various roles to five other students who remain in the room: a doctor, a politician, a used-car salesman, a priest, a bus driver, or something similar to these roles. These students will shake the hands of the students outside who will try to guess the role of each person. Their guesses will be based on the handshakes and facial expressions. Mention that it would be rare for someone to guess the precise role being played; if the guess is close, it should be counted as a correct guess.

4. Conduct another simple role-playing exercise to demonstrate the characteristics of the id, ego, and superego. Assign someone to be an id, another to be an ego, and another to be a superego. Have them play out a situation that involves conflict: "I want to eat that chocolate cake, but I better not; I want to ask him out, but I better not; I want to yell at her, but I better not." Remind them that the three-part dialogue theoretically occurs in one's mind. Afterwards, point out the accuracy or the inaccuracy of some of the lines used during the role-playing.

5. It might be interesting to compare two social psychoanalysts, Horney and Adler, to one humanist, Maslow. Maslow's hierarchy of needs takes into account both Horney's emphasis on love (Maslow's third level) and Adler's emphasis on feeling worthwhile (Maslow's fourth level). For Maslow, both concerns are essential, but one need must be satisfied before the other. Ask students if they agree with this particular assumption. What if they could satisfy only one of these needs? Which would they choose?

One final note: The beginning of the chapter discusses the usefulness of theories. Point out that Maslow certainly knew of Horney's and Adler's theories, and these theories were possibly USEFUL to him in some direct or indirect way when he developed his own theory. This may explain why Maslow's theory seems more encompassing than Horney's and Adler's. In other words, some theories are useful because they inspire other theories.

6. To point out the complexity of modeling, discuss the various ways that high school freshmen model themselves after seniors. Students may have difficulty at first recalling specific behaviors that THEY "copied" as freshmen, but a little prompting may jar their memories: "Imagine freshman year. What kinds of things did seniors do that were cool? Did they walk or hold their books in a particular way? Did they hang out in certain places or sit in a particular area of the cafeteria? Did they wear cool clothes? Was there anything about their lockers that was cool? What about the way they talked?" If you can get students to describe ten or fifteen concrete examples of modeling, your point that modeling is a complex process should hit home. If this process is complex at school, imagine how complex it is at home!

15 Measuring Personality

A. CHAPTER OUTLINE

- **WHY TESTS ARE USED**
  - Psychological Tests

- **MAKING A PERSONALITY TEST**
  - Establishing Norms
  - Establishing Validity
  - Establishing Reliability

- **PERSONALITY INVENTORIES**
  - California Psychological Inventory

- **PROJECTIVE TESTS**
  - Rorschach Test (Ink Blot Test)
  - Principle of Projection

- **APTITUDE AND ACHIEVEMENT TESTS**
  - Aptitude Tests
    - Mechanical Comprehension
    - Verbal Skills
    - Clerical Speed and Accuracy
  - Achievement Tests
    - SAT

- **VOCATIONAL INTEREST TESTS**
  - Strong-Campbell Interest Inventory
  - Cautions about Interest Tests

- **SECOND LOOK AT TEST VALIDITY**

- **ALTERNATIVES TO TESTING**
  - Interviews
    - Halo Effect
    - Reverse Halo Effect
    - Standoutishness
  - Situational Assessments

- **ETHICS OF TESTING**

B) TEXTBOOK DISCUSSION QUESTIONS

1. *You may have filled out a personality inventory or two in your lifetime, but you were probably never made aware of your score. Why do you suppose scores are not made more readily available? Explain.*

   The scores, if made readily available, may be misinterpreted by nonprofessionals. Even if the scores ARE interpreted correctly, the nonprofessional may exaggerate the importance of the test, not realizing perhaps that no test is perfect.

2. *As stated in the first question, most of us aren't aware of our scores on personality inventories that we may have taken in the past. Should this information be made more easily available? For example, should personality inventory scores be routinely sent out in the mail? Why or why not? Explain.*

   Reasoning may vary slightly, but most students will probably agree that the scores should NOT be made easily available. Two possible reasons are listed in #1 above. Another problem might involve students comparing scores and ridiculing those with "low" scores.

3. *A reliable personality inventory should paint a somewhat accurate picture of various personality traits. What trait would a personality inventory have an easier time identifying: honesty or shyness? In other words, Joe fills out a personality inventory; if you (as an expert) were to analyze his answers, would it be easier to draw conclusions about whether he is honest or whether he is shy? Explain.*

   Accept any answers that are logically supported. The chapter mentions techniques that professionals use to "catch" liars. For example, a professional may ask essentially the same question in five or six different parts of the test, varying the wording, then noting whether the test taker is consistent in his or her answers each time. Could someone overcome these traps? Maybe. Shyness is probably more elusive than lying and harder to measure and identify. Someone may be shy in one situation, but may become bold when taking tests, for example.

4. *In your opinion, do students attempt to achieve a halo effect more often during junior high school or high school? Why? Does it have anything to do with peers?*

   This is another one of those questions where students will point out how OTHER students attempt to achieve a halo effect, but will deny that THEY themselves ever attempt the same. After discussing which kinds of students are more guilty of trying to achieve a halo effect (junior high or high school?) and after discussing HOW this halo effect is achieved by students, confront them with this denial.

5. *Describe several experimental situations where researchers would want to use situational assessment rather than an interview. Remember that the problem with interviewing or asking questions is that the answers may not be truthful or accurate; also, once someone knows that he or she is being tested, that person's behavior automatically tends to become less natural.*

Possible situations where situational assessment might be preferred:

    a) You want to find out how children play with each other and how this affects development;

    b) You want to find out when or why people will help in an emergency, so you stage an emergency and observe.

    c) You want to find out the effects of mild stress on job performance.

In all of the above situations, if the subjects know they are being observed or tested, their behavior may become less than natural.

C) TEXTBOOK ACTIVITIES

1. Keep in mind that many counselors are former teachers who might welcome the opportunity to visit a class to talk about these testing issues!

2. If students have difficulty finding information on personality and achievement tests, mention that their counselors and school psychologist probably have a great deal of information about these topics.

3. Students should have fun with these activities. If you decide not to assign these activities, consider conducting them during class time by sending students around the school or to the cafeteria to collect data. Tally and analyze this data when they return.

4. If students conduct all the activities for this chapter, their counselors will be kept busy! After completing the interest test, some students may complain that they do not know anyone in the three occupations in which they scored highest. Mention that they can find an appropriate person in the telephone book and that they can conduct at least a brief interview over the telephone.

IN-CLASS ACTIVITIES / LESSON SUGGESTIONS

1. To introduce the chapter, create three or four ink blots similar to those shown in the chapter. (An art teacher at your school may be willing to help.) Display the ink blots in class and announce that you are going to analyze some of their personalities. Ask for a volunteer to come to the front of the room to closely examine each ink blot. After viewing each ink blot, the volunteer should report what he or she sees. Make a note of the responses; you might even want to pretend that you are timing how long it takes to respond. Repeat this entire procedure on three of four other students.

   Afterwards, open this manual to this page and pretend that you are carefully comparing their responses to a list or a key of possible responses which, in turn, will reveal a "Professional Analysis of Personality." Insist that it has taken years of research to arrive at these professional analyses. Here are some "professional" analyses that you can use:

   1) You are definitely a "people-person." If given a complex research task to complete, you will more likely ask friends for their advice rather than going to the library. You would be miserable if you had a job where you had to sit behind a desk all day.

   2) You feel that your biggest problem in your life right now is a lack of confidence. There have been times in your past that you've felt confident, but right now you find it difficult to recapture that feeling.

   3) You are often skeptical and even suspicious of other people's intentions. Even when you get to know someone well, you still worry that this person will betray you or hurt you in some way.

   4) Your most admirable trait is your persistence. Even when you hear others complain, you do not allow it to affect you. You don't always achieve what you want, but you persevere and you're proud of this quality.

   5) You are an extrovert who sometimes regrets being so outgoing. You worry that others misinterpret your bold comments, but you can't control yourself; you can't keep your mouth shut.

   6) You tend to be a quiet person. It's not that you do not have anything to say, but you worry that others may be judging you.

   Be creative in matching these "analyses" with student responses. Try to create at least a minimal degree of plausibility. For example, if someone sees a spider, perhaps use analysis #3.

   At this point in the course, your savvy students may see through your charade, which is okay. Have them point out what they perceive to be the problems with your ink blot analyses. Most likely, these problems will coincide with the problems listed in the text. Regardless of their answers, this discussion should provide a lead-in to the material on norms, validity, reliability, and projective tests. Explain what these concepts mean and relate them to the ink blot test. Ask if there are any ways to make the ink blot test more reliable and valid. For example, what if the test included multiple choices (which would make it less projective)? What if the test were used along with other tests? What if the test were administered to the same person over a period of months—would this make it more reliable? Is it possible to establish norms for projective tests?

2. Here's another activity to clarify the projective-test philosophy. Have students bring in a picture that represents their personalities. For example, if a student is highly motivated and ambitious, this person might bring in a picture of a locomotive, white smoke billowing out of its stack. The pictures should represent their personalities, not their interests. For example, someone who enjoys hockey should not bring in something so obvious as a picture of a hockey player. Explain that they should not show anyone their pictures. In fact, have them (at home) tape their pictures onto a piece of loose leaf paper to make everyone's pictures more uniform. Collect the pictures face-down, mix them up, and tape them onto the chalkboard. These pictures will be their "projections" of their personalities. (The pictures may not be projections in the strict sense of the term, but for the sake of this activity, assume that students' choices of pictures reflect their innermost self.)

    Go through each picture and have the class try to develop a brief profile of the person who brought in the picture. Is the person male or female? Extroverted or introverted? Cautious or easy-going? You can even have the class guess the identity of the person who brought in the picture. Under each picture, write down some of the class's responses. Afterwards, go back to each picture and have the owner of each remark on how accurate the profile was. Some of the profiles may be remarkably accurate! Point out, however, that the profiles were made by friends and acquaintances. Would an objective outsider have developed the same profiles? If the profiles are not that accurate, this should demonstrate how difficult it is to measure personality through an open-ended test such as this one.

3. Use **MASTERS 15-2** and **15-3** to conduct textbook Activity #4 in class. Pass out one of these masters to half of your students and the other master to the other.half.

4. Like Chapter 2, this chapter includes material that is not as inherently interesting to students as material in other chapters. Therefore, you may want to move this chapter along at a brisk pace. Consider inviting a counselor or your school psychologist to class to discuss how they use tests, how students can prepare for achievement tests, how reliable and valid personality and aptitude and vocational interest tests are. If they can't visit, maybe they can give you some sample tests to administer to your students.

    Here's an address of a company that may be able to supply you with tests:
    Consulting Psychologists Press, Inc., 577 College Ave, Palo Alto, Calif. 94306

16 Frustration, Conflict, Stress & Drugs

A. CHAPTER OUTLINE

- **FRUSTRATION**
- **CONFLICT**
    - Approach-Approach Conflict
    - Approach-Avoidance Conflict
    - Avoidance-Avoidance Conflict
    - Double Approach-Avoidance Conflict
- **ANXIETY**
- **STRESS**
    - Good Stress
    - Bad Stress
    - Physical Changes With Stress
        - Fight or Flight Reaction
        - Human Response (Stress Hormone)
    - Examining Stress
        - Pushing. Too Hard
        - Personal Attitude
    - Stress and Personality
        - Unrelieved Tension
        - Personality Types (A and B)
        - General Adaptation Syndrome
            - Alarm Reaction
            - Stage of Resistance
            - Exhaustion
- **SUBSTANCE OR CHEMICAL ABUSE**
    - How Drugs Work
    - Alcohol
        - Chemical Effects
        - Physical Effects
            - Alcoholic Withdrawal Delirium
            - Hallucinations
        - Synergistic Effect
        - Causes of Alcoholism
        - Indicators of Alcoholism
        - Alcoholism as a Disease
    - Marijuana (Psychedelic)
    - Amphetamines
        - Tolerance
    - Cocaine
        - Psychological Dependence
    - Opiates
        - Physical Dependence
    - LSD (Hallucinogen)
    - Steroids
- **SUICIDE**
    - Common Stresses
    - Teenage Suicide

B) TEXTBOOK DISCUSSION QUESTIONS

1. *If you had to create a chart similar to the Social Readjustment Rating Scale, which would you rank as more stressful: moving to a new school or breaking up with a boyfriend or girlfriend whom you have been dating for two months? Explain.*

Answers will vary.

2-3. *If someone followed you around with a video camera from the beginning of this school year to the present—and only filmed you at school—what conclusions would a person viewing the video draw about your personality? Would your behavior indicate a type A or a type B personality? Explain. Note: Conclusions should be based only on your behavior, not on your thoughts.*

   Answer the question in number 2, but this time, imagine someone is reading only your thoughts and not seeing any behavior. What conclusions would be drawn in this case? Explain.

Consider using these topics as in-class journal entries and then asking for volunteers to read their entries aloud.

4. *As noted in the chapter, the general adaption syndrome isn't going to apply to every stressful situation. We have all experienced, at one time or another, however, each of these stages. If you found out that you had to get a tooth pulled in three hours, which state would you probably experience more intensely in the next three hours, the alarm stage or the stage of resistance? Explain.*

People who are extremely squeamish will most likely experience the alarm stage more intensely. Instead of resisting the attack, these people may simply panic and remain "alarmed." Those less squeamish will get beyond the alarm stage and allow their bodies to "resist" more readily and more intensely.

5. *You are probably familiar with the theory that one of the reasons young people drink alcohol is that it is illegal or forbidden. Do you think this reason applies to the young drinkers in your area? Why or why not? Explain.*

Answers will vary. If students agree that the illegality of alcohol promotes drinking, why doesn't this hold true for other illegal behaviors? Burglary, for example, is illegal, yet this illegality does not make burglary an attractive possibility for most people. This logic is simple and perhaps the analogy is not quite fair, but it should lead to the idea that there are numerous reasons why young people drink. Discuss these reasons.

6. *It should be fairly obvious to you how advertisers glorify alcohol use. Some people claim that this type of glorification has little effect on nondrinkers, that it will not significantly alter drinking habits. Furthermore, the purpose of the ads is to promote or highlight a particular brand name, not drinking in general. Others argue that the constant barrage of alcohol ads certainly does affect drinking habits. The ads send the message that it is perfectly acceptable to drink. With which argument do you tend to agree and why? Explain.*

Answers will vary. It might be interesting to compare their answers to the behavioral and humanistic approaches discussed in earlier chapters. A behaviorist would probably argue that the association of alcohol with positive images certainly would condition us to respond positively to alcohol. A humanist might argue that we are not so easily swayed by 60-second spots on TV; our decision to drink or not drink will be based more on internal motivations.

7. *As stated in the previous question, advertisers explicitly condone alcohol consumption. Some would argue that not only do advertisers promote this drug use but also our society as a whole condones the use of alcohol and other kinds of drugs. What are some of the subtle ways in which our society says it is all right to use drugs? Explain.*

Discuss this question in class. See In-Class Activity #6 for ideas.

8. *As noted in the chapter, the press often plays up suicide. Should there be restrictions on what the press can report when a suicide occurs? Why or why not? Explain.*

Those who want restrictions on the press may argue that widespread coverage tends to glorify suicide. Some restrictions may include the following: a)The dead person's face should not be flashed on the nightly news or printed in the newspaper; b) The method of suicide should not be explained; c) The dead person's friends should not be hounded with questions by reporters.

C) TEXTBOOK ACTIVITIES

1. If you want to create ONE good chart that the entire class can use to collect data elsewhere, have everyone make a chart and combine the best from all of them. Or brainstorm for ideas in class and create a chart right there! Warn students that their analyses should be as specific as possible. As the chapter suggests, one cannot simply add the scores and predict illness. Students should compare major stressors (as well as overall scores) to illness.

2. If you do not assign this activity, consider conducting it on your students, comparing one class to another.

3. Students are often extremely creative with this kind of activity. If you do not assign this activity, perhaps you can have each student bring in two pictures, one that glorifies drugs and one that shows the reality of drugs. With these pictures you can decorate the entire room or just a bulletin board or two.

4. Have students add their own questions to the ones already listed in the text.

5. Students should have no difficulty finding information on these topics.

6. You may want to have students share their information with the class. The information may one day come in handy for them, either directly or indirectly.

D) IN-CLASS ACTIVITIES / LESSON SUGGESTIONS

1. Here's a fun activity to demonstrate a particular aspect of frustration. Your hypothesis will be this: If people know ahead of time that they will be frustrated, and if they understand the nature of this frustration, they will FEEL less frustrated than people without this knowledge or understanding. In other words, people who wait in line to buy tickets and who know that the wait will be thirty minutes will experience less frustration than people who wait in the same line without this information.

To test this hypothesis, ask for two volunteers and have these students leave the room. Explain the hypothesis to the rest of the class and announce that you're going to play a game to test the hypothesis. Place about twelve sheets of paper in a sort of line on the floor, each sheet representing one "move." The first sheet in the line should say "START"; the last sheet should say "FINISH"; the other sheets can be blank. The goal of the game is for players to move from START to FINISH. Players will be given a deck of note-cards that you will prepare which will instruct them whether to move forward or not. The player who reaches FINISH using the fewest cards wins. Your players, in this case, will be your two volunteers. As will be explained in a moment, both players will experience frustration during the game, but only one of the players will be informed beforehand about this frustration.

Invite in the first player (the informed subject) and "read" these instructions: "Imagine that the sheets on the floor are part of a game board. Your goal is to move from START to FINISH, using the fewest number of these playing cards as possible. The playing cards will tell you when to move forward and back. If you have used fewer cards than _____ (the other player) by the time you reach FINISH, you win. The winner will receive _____."

Have a prize ready for the winner: an apple, a candy bay, extra credit points. A small incentive may serve to create some real frustration. Continue reading the following to the first player (but only to the first player):

"You'll notice as you pick the cards that quite a few of them will say, 'Go back to START.' In fact, twelve of the cards say this! In other words, you would have to be extremely lucky to get to FINISH by the time you finish the deck. If you do NOT reach FINISH by the end of the deck, we'll reshuffle the cards and continue playing with REVISED RULES. When we go through the cards this second time, we'll assume that all the cards that say, 'Go back to START' really say, 'Do not move forward.' These cards then will have no effect on your progress." (Shuffle the cards and hand them over. Keep track of the used cards; one way is to have them hand the used cards to you.)

As should be clear by now, you will need to prepare about 35 index cards. You can do it in the following manner:

# OF CARDS	INSTRUCTIONS
15	"Move forward one"
12	"Go back to START"
2	"Move forward two"
1	"Move forward three"
1	"Move forward four"
3	"Move back two"
1	"Move back three"

As the first player plays the game, your other students should be jotting down their informal observations on the player's frustration level. Does the player swear, sigh, slap a desk? If you want to make these observations more formal, have a few students actually count the number of sighs, and so on. After the first player reaches FINISH, invite in the second player and repeat the above procedure, but do NOT explain how many cards say "Go back." Once all the cards have been used, you WILL have to explain the revised rules to the second player. Again, other students should jot down their observations. Afterwards, compare observations and discuss the hypothesis. Who was more frustrated? What particular aspect of the game caused the most frustration?

Consider using more than two players, simply so students have more to observe. Keep in mind that players do not need to be part of your class. As people stroll by your classroom, you can drag them in, or you can pull in people from study hall! Another thing you can do to ensure that your students have enough to observe is somehow have your players face the class while playing the game; you can move the desks aside and place START in the front of the room and FINISH in the back. Finally, have players read the cards aloud so that the class can also observe verbal behavior.

Discussion. Regardless of your "results," discuss the frustration involved in waiting in line. WHY is waiting in line so frustrating? Are some types of lines better than others? What kinds of things make waiting in line LESS frustrating? For example, Disneyland often posts a waiting time for many of its rides. Does this help? Would it help to somehow post the waiting time during traffic jams (which many radio stations try to do during rush hours)? What if you are told that you have to wait 30 minutes, at a restaurant for instance, and you wait 60 minutes and are still not seated? Does this make you more frustrated than if you were told nothing at all?

2. Consider trying variations of the game described above. For example, you can frustrate your players even more by timing them. Or you can have two players playing at the same time. Or you can write various instructions on the sheets on the floor. After conducting this activity in class, ask your students to think of other variations.

3. Break the class into small groups and have each group think of a creative example for each of the four conflicts described in the chapter. After 5-10 minutes, have each group report their examples to the rest of the class. Consider offering a prize for the most creative group: a candy bar, extra credit points, the option of not having to complete the next MINOR assignment. This last prize is usually highly valued. Warn them that the examples must be not only creative but accurate as well.

4. The differences between a Type A and a Type B personality is not a difficult one to grasp. However, students can probably use an exercise or two to bring these concepts to life. There are several ways to do this. One, get two people to role-play a conversation between a Type A and a Type B person. Two, have students write a journal entry from the point of view of either a Type A or a Type B person. Three, have students identify how their own personalities may be primarily Type A or Type B. See the December 1988 issue of PSYCHOLOGY TODAY for a Health Personality Test and an article on the topic.

Possible journal topics:

    a) Your teacher has just announced that a major term paper is due in a month.

    b) You can get tickets to a concert for tomorrow, but you have to work.

    c) You have just received a rejection letter for admission from the college of your choice.

Possible role-playing situations. (Students can decide which character will be "A" and which will be "B.")

    a) A husband and a wife are discussing whether they should have a baby.

    b) Two students are trying to decide if they should join a team at school.

    c) Two family members are discussing where they should go on vacation.

5. Have students use textbook Discussion Question #6 to conduct an informal survey. They need to find five people who drink and five people who do not drink to answer the question. Collect everyone's data and see if you can draw any conclusions. A possible hypothesis is this: Nondrinkers will argue that the ads DO affect drinking habits (but THEY are strong enough to resist this influence); drinkers will argue that the ads have little or no effect on drinking habits (THEY drink because they choose to drink).

6. Introduce the section on drugs by writing this on the board: "It's OK to use drugs." Have students think of numerous ways that our society promotes this message. You can either do this together as a class or allow students to work in small groups. Possible ways that our society promotes drug use:

    A) Alcohol commercials and ads (Have them think of numerous slogans.)

    B) Events sponsored by alcohol manufacturers: football games, concerts, and so on.

    C) Commercials and ads for aspirin and other pain relievers

    D) TV shows—past and present (Have them think of specific references to drugs.)

    E) Movies (Again, specific references?)

    F) Radio station disc-jockeys (Specific references?)

    G) Parents (Do their parties ALWAYS include alcohol?)

    H) Friends

You might point out that the very nature of our society may promote drug use. For instance, we expect fast-service, instant food, instant relief. It's no wonder then that some people use drugs, believing that the drugs will not only relieve physical pain, but psychological pain as well.

7. This chapter provides another opportunity for a visit from a speaker. Contact a drug and alcohol rehab center in your area. These centers typically have several staff members who are eager to visit high school classes; in some cases, speaking to groups is the main responsibility of these particular staff members.

17 Toward a Healthy Personality

A. CHAPTER OUTLINE

■ BODY-MIND INTERACTIONS
  Cognitive and Psysical
  Sudden Death Phenomenom
  Issue of Control

■ COPING WITH BODILY STRESSES
  Immune System
  Antibodies
  Ulcers
  Asthma
  Headaches
      Muscle Contraction Headaches
      Migraine Headaches

■ PAIN AND PAIN CONTROL
  Phantom-Limb Pain
  Subjective Pain
  Chemical Relief
      Endorphins
  Placebo Effect
  Pain and Mental Processes
  Rerouting Nerve Impulses
  Acupuncture

■ CONTROLLING THOUGHTS
  Cognitive Strategies
      Distraction
      Redefinition
  Biofeedback

■ PSYCHOLOGICAL DEFENSE MECHANISMS
  Repression
  Rationalization
  Projection
  Regression
  Denial
  Why We Use Defense Mechanisms

B) TEXTBOOK DISCUSSION QUESTIONS

1. *Imagine you are locked for an hour in a room in which a virus has been released into the atmosphere. Do you believe that there are any mental strategies you could use to prevent the virus from entering your body? If so, what kinds of strategies would you use? If not, why not? Explain.*

   Can mental strategies prevent a virus from entering the body? Opinions will vary. Most students will probably agree that the brain, in theory, is powerful enough to block the virus. Asked if THEY could block the virus, most students will be less confident about THEIR own abilities. The implicit lesson here is that mental strategies CAN be learned and developed. What KIND of strategies might work in this case? Students could argue that distraction and redefinition may help. Or they might suggest some sort of visualization where the person could imagine fighting off the virus with imaginary shields. How much all this will help is questionable, of course.

2. *The chapter explains that sudden death phenomenon occurs because of a person's cognitive outlook: The person believes he or she will die. Do you think that a person can literally kill himself or herself, not only because of beliefs but also because of a desire to die? In other words, can a person wish to die and, simply through wishing, actually die? Explain.*

   Students may be able to provide examples of people who have "willed" themselves to death. For example, if a woman dies in February, the husband may become so distraught that he dies the following month.

3. *We all experience times when we feel that we have little control over circumstances. Do you tend to feel this way more often at school or at home? Explain.*

   Answers will vary.

4. *If you found out today that: (1) many people who get ulcers feel helpless and lack control over their environment and (2) that you had an ulcer, would you change anything about your life-style? If so, what specifically would you change? If not, why not? Explain.*

   Answers will vary. Those who feel a lack of control over their environments would probably NOT change their lifestyles; these people probably feel that they CANNOT do anything to change it!

5. *If you suffered from migraine headaches and you could eliminate these headaches either by taking medication for the rest of your life or by undergoing an intensive five-days-a-week, yearlong training program in biofeedback, which would you choose and why?*

   Students' answers will relate again to their loci of control. Those who feel that they have little control over their lives will probably opt to take medicine, not believing that THEY can do anything about their headaches.

B) TEXTBOOK DISCUSSION QUESTIONS, Continued

6. *Let's say that five years ago you suffered from severe headaches. Your doctor, however, prescribed pills that virtually eliminated these headaches. If the pills that the doctor prescribed were, in fact, placebos, would you now want to know this? Why or why not? Explain.*

This is a good question to discuss in class. Some students may not want to know out of fear that the headaches will then return. These people probably feel that they have little internal control over their lives. The ones who would want to know probably feel that they DO have great internal control over their lives; knowing about the placebos then would reaffirm these ideas.

7. *If it is true that responses to some pain must be learned, what have you learned about pain and from whom have you learned it? Discuss.*

Students need to be creative with this question. They can describe their reactions to painful visits with the doctor and the dentist and compare these visits to how their parents react to pain.

8. *The chapter mentions that the success of acupuncture depends, to some extent, on the patient's expectations. With this in mind, would acupuncture ever work on you? Why or why not? Explain.*

Again, answers may relate to students' beliefs in their loci of control. Before discussing any of the discussion questions for this chapter, it might be a good idea to have students fill out the Locus of Control Scale from the chapter.

C) TEXTBOOK ACTIVITIES

1. If you feel that it's worthwhile, you might have students read an entire book rather than just twenty pages. This might be especially appropriate if your school offers a Psychology 2 course or Independent Study in psychology.

2. Consider inviting to your class one or two of the people that your students find.

3-4. These activities require some extra preparation and assistance from other teachers, but the results should be worthwhile. The activites are compelling demonstrations of the power of suggestion. If suggestion can influence a fundamental thing like the perception of smell, perhaps suggestion (through a placebo) can affect the body's healing processes.

5. Students should have no difficulty finding information on these topics.

6-7. Share the best of these songs and posters with the rest of the class.

D) IN-CLASS ACTIVITIES / LESSON SUGGESTIONS

1. Try to bring into class a biofeedback machine to demonstrate the nearly immediate and practical benefits of biofeedback. Contact a local electronics store and you can probably buy a simple biofeedback device for under $20. Or if you have an electronics course at your school, the teacher may be able to give you some advice on how to build one. Better yet, convince this person to have his or her students build one.

2. You might point out that some people who claim to have extraordinary mind-body powers are really charlatans. For example, ANYONE can sit on a bed of nails or walk across a bed of hot coals. If you know what you're doing, you can even stick your hand into a pot of boiling lead. Ask your physics teacher at school why these feats are possible and for ideas on other not-so-remarkable feats.

3. The American Dental Association had an article which quoted AMERICAN HEALTH MAGAZINE which, in turn, quoted THE JOURNAL OF THE CANADIAN DENTAL ASSOCIATION, claiming that there was a study which showed that putting ice cubes on the web of the hand between the thumb and first finger will greatly reduce or eliminate pain from a toothache. We have no way of knowing if it works, but given the history of acupuncture, there is always the possibility that it might. Try it. The worst that can happen is a cold hand.

4. Here's a simple and fun activity to review the different types of defense mechanisms. Have two students leave the room and have them choose a defense mechanism while waiting outside. Meanwhile, the class should pick a situation: a husband and a wife are walking to a train station; a boss is discussing a work schedule with an employee; and so on. The two students outside should then return and act out the situation, one or both of them using the defense mechanism that they chose. For example, the employee in the situation above could use denial to explain an unexplained absence at work. The rest of the class should try to guess which defense mechanism is being used.

18 Behavior Disorders

A. CHAPTER OUTLINE

■ NATURE OF BEHAVIOR DISORDERS
  Definitions of Behavior Disorders
  Nonpsychotic Versus Psychotic Disorders

■ CHARACTERISTICS OF NONPSYCHOTIC DISORDERS

■ CLASSIFYING DISORDERS—DSM III

■ ANXIETY DISORDERS
  Panic Disorder
  Phobic Disorders
        Simple Phobia
        Agoraphobia
  Obsessions and Compulsions

■ DISSOCIATIVE DISORDERS
  Psychogenic Amnesia
        Selective Forgetting
  Multiple Personality

■ DYSTHYMIC DISORDER

■ CHARACTERISTICS OF PSYCHOTIC DISORDERS
  Thought Disorders
  Hallucinations
  Delusions
  Inappopriate Emotions

■ MAJOR AFFECTIVE DISORDERS
  Major Depression
  Mania
  Flight of Ideas
  Bipolar Disorder

■ SCHIZOPHRENIC DISORDERS
  Word Salad
  Clang Associations
  Psychotic Episodes
  Incidence of Schizophrenia
  Chemical Factors in Schizophrenia
        Dopamine

■ PERSONALITY DISORDERS
  Antisocial Personality Disorder (Sociopath)

B) TEXTBOOK DISCUSSION QUESTIONS

1. *Other than violent behaviors, list five behaviors that our society would consider abnormal. Then, for each of the five behaviors, describe a situation where the abnormal behavior might be considered normal. For example, eating another human is certainly regarded as abnormal, but, if this happened three weeks after a plane crash in which the person had died and the survivors were stranded, the behavior could be construed by many as normal.*

   Listed below are possible "abnormal" behaviors, followed by situations where the behaviors might be considered normal:
   a) talking to yourself — while praying
   b) walking around nearly nude — at the beach
   c) gambling EVERY day — and you win
   d) standing in the middle of the street waving your arms wildly — and you are a traffic cop

2. *If a high school student has been drinking alcohol for a year and has gotten drunk every weekend-but only on weekends-should this person get help from a professional? Yes? No? Depends? Explain.*

   You may be surprised at students' answers. Some may argue that yes, the person should seek help since the alcohol is clearly in control. Others may argue no, that the person only uses alcohol on weekends, that it doesn't disrupt the person's life. The best answer would probably be that it depends. How does the person react to the alcohol? Does the person become violent toward him- or herself or others? If so, the person should definitely seek help. If not, perhaps the person does not need professional help. The person may still need to quit drinking for other obvious reasons— damage to the liver, and so on—but professional help MAY not be necessary.

3. *Courts today still sometimes use the verdict of "not guilty by reason of insanity." The logic here is that the person was unaware of his or her actions and should not be held responsible. Most likely, the person who is awarded this verdict will be committed to a mental institution until psychiatrists determine that the person is "sane"-at which time, the person will be released. Do you agree that this type of verdict should be allowed, or should "insane" criminals be treated just like any other criminals? Explain.*

   This is an interesting question to discuss in class. The crux of the issue seems to be this: CAN psychiatrists accurately determine the state of a person's mental health? They may be able to determine mental health on a short-term basis, but can they predict future mental health? Even on a short-term basis, CAN psychiatrists avoid being duped by patients who fake mental health?

4. *Why would it be unlikely that a person suffering from a personality disorder would be awarded a verdict of "not guilty by reason of insanity"? Explain.*

   People with peronality disorders are in touch with reality. They understand the consequences of their actions. They simply have no conscience to guide their actions.

5. **If someone had an intense fear of water, which of the following "solutions" would be most effective in reducing the fear: letting the person gradually get used to the water or throwing the person into the water and letting him or her confront the fear all at one time? Explain. Which method would you prefer and why?**

    Either method MAY work, though throwing someone into the water may backfire and evoke more fear. Which method would be more effective? Effectiveness will vary, depending on the person's personality, age, and fear level.

6. **Describe a simple phobia that you have. As noted in the chapter, this simple phobia is probably the result of learning. You may not have ever thought about it, but make several guesses as to how you learned this simple phobia.**

    Answers will vary.

7. **If a person supposedly suffering from multiple personality committed a felony and his or her lawyer pleaded not guilty by reason of insanity, what are several ways that you might be able to determine whether the alleged criminal is truly suffering from the disorder or faking it? Explain.**

    You might measure the person's brain waves with an EEG. There seems to be evidence that each personality of a multiple personality evokes unique EEG patterns. You might also try other methods of measuring brain activity—like PET scans or CAT scans. Or you might secretly film the person to observe "natural" behavior.

8. **We have all suffered mild bouts of depression from time to time, but we usually snap out of it in a relatively short time. Let's say that you had a friend who was more than mildly depressed. What kind of advice would you give this person to help him or her snap out of the depression (not that we necessarily recommend you actually offer this advice)**

    Answers will vary. The advice that students think of will probably be the same "advice" that they give themselves when depressed. Chapter 19 discusses the importance of analyzing this self-advice (or these internalized sentences).

C) TEXTBOOK ACTIVITIES

1. The directions for this activity should be self-explanatory. Just make sure to explain what ECT is before assigning it. (See Chapter 19.)

2. Students should have no difficulties finding information on this topic. Tell them to consider contacting a mental institution for information.

3. Again, students should have no difficulty finding information on this topic.

4-5. Students may want to add other phobias to the ones already listed in the activity. They can refer to the In-Focus section on phobias for ideas. Also, they may want to add an "other" category.

6. Since this section includes three activities that require research, consider bringing your class to the library for a class period to gather information.

D) IN-CLASS ACTIVITIES / LESSON SUGGESTIONS

1. Students often have many misconceptions about behavior disorders, the foremost being that there is a clear-cut disctinction between "abnormal" and "normal." While the distinction may be clear-cut between two particular individuals at a certain point in time, the distinction often becomes hazy and ambiguous at another time or for two other individuals. To demonstrate this ambiguity, simply act "crazy" while discussing the definitions of behavior disorders. Knock over desks, talk to the pencil sharpener, put your left shoe on your right foot. Meanwhile, ask questions: What is normal? What is abnormal? If someone puts his left shoe on his right foot, is this normal? Is it—is it? Huh—huh? And so on. You'll get plenty of laughs, but you'll also get some inspiring conclusions. For example, "normal" depends on the situation, on the culture in which the behavior occurs, and so on. Point out the three criteria for "abnormal" listed in the text: 1) the person suffers discomfort; 2) the person behaves in a bizarre way; 3) the person is highly inefficient. Afterwards, explain that your "craziness" was not a mockery, that you were not trying to make light of people with serious disorders. You were just trying to illustrate a point!

2. Students enjoy reading or hearing about real cases of behavior disorders. The text includes several case-study examples, but you can easily find more in a text on abnormal psychology. You can either present these real examples as you go along to satisfy students' interests, or you can use them at the end of the chapter for review. If you do the latter, present the examples, but describe only the symptoms, and students can try to identify the disorders described.

3. While reading the chapter, students may often find themselves identifying with the symptoms of one disorder or another. Reassure them that this is common and that this alone does not mean that they have the disorder. To illustrate this, YOU may want to share with students the symptoms of a disorder with which you identify. What are your phobias and compulsions?

4. Since depression is so common, spend some time allowing students to explain why they get depressed and how they overcome it. Consider putting them in a circle to promote a certain degree of openness and intimacy. This is not meant as a therapy session, but the discussion may help some of them realize the universality of depression.

5. Use **MASTERS** 18-2 and 18-3 to conduct textbook Activity #1 in class. Pass out one of the masters to half the class and the other master to the other half. Note that "electroconvulsive" therapy has been changed to "electroshock" therapy, a more familiar term to students. This should avoid questions about the term during class, questions that will confuse the "divorce" control group and that will ruin the experiment. While handing out the masters, you may even want to insist that no questions be asked.

6. If you have any kind of mental health center near your school, try to take a field trip there. No matter how much book-knowledge students absorb, they may never overcome their misconceptions about mental illness without such a visit. Besides, it's fascinating. One misconception that students may have about the VISIT is that you will be able to walk through the wards and gawk at the patients. Not likely. However, state hospitals regularly conduct open hearings to decide which patients can and cannot be released, which is riveting—and real. Perhaps you can arrange to attend one of these hearings. If you do attend, your students will realize how important the DSM-III manual is. It, along with the judge, essentially determines who stays in the hospital and who is released.

19 Treatment and Therapy

A. CHAPTER OUTLINE

■ MENTAL HEALTH THROUGH THE YEARS
  Philippe Pinel

■ TYPES OF MENTAL HEALTH WORKERS
  Psychologists
    Counseling Psychologists
    Clinical Psychologists
  Psychiatrists
  Other Mental Health Personnel
    Psychiatric Social Worker
    Psychiatric Nurses
  Psychotherapists—The Blanket Term

■ PSYCHOANALYTIC TREATMENT
  Free Association
  Transference

■ HUMANISTIC THERAPY
    Client-Centered Therapy (Non-Directive Therapy)
    Unconditional Positive Regard

■ BEHAVIORAL THERAPY
  Systematic Desensitization
  Aversive Conditioning
  Token Economy

■ COGNITIVE BEHAVIORAL THERAPY

■ GROUP THERAPY
  The Group Method
  Encounter Therapy

■ COMMONALITIES OF THERAPY

■ EFFECTIVENESS OF THERAPY

■ CHEMOTHERAPY

■ ELECTROCONVULSIVE SHOCK THERAPY

■ PSYCHOSURGERY

■ CONTROVERSY: MENTAL ILLNESS

B) TEXTBOOK DISCUSSION QUESTIONS

1. *What kinds of problems would be better dealt with using psychoanalysis, and which problems would be better dealt with using behavioral therapy? Explain.*

Psychoanalysis may be a better treatment for deep seated, complex problems stemming perhaps from child abuse or neglect or some other severe trauma. Theoretically, this abuse will cause resentment and guilt that will eventually be repressed. Psychoanalysis will theoretically helps bring this resentment and guilt to the surface so it can be resolved. Behavioral therapy may be a better treatment for eliminating or reducing specific behaviors that interfere with day-to-day living. These behaviors can range from simple bad habits, like smoking or mildly overeating, to more severe problems, like never eating or washing one's hands 500 times a day.

2. *Describe a person, in your past or present, who consistently has demonstrated unconditional positive regard toward you. What effect, if any, did (or does) this have on you? Explain.*

Answers will vary.

3. *If your principal wanted to incorporate a token economy system at your school, what are several ways in which to do this? Be specific. Do you think adopting your suggestions would realistically have any effect on students' behaviors? Explain.*

The principal would first have to decide which behaviors will be rewarded—which raises questions about the ethics of behaviorism. Why should the principal get to decide? If not the principal, then who? In other words, who determines what is "desired" behavior? Consider discussing these ethical issues in class.

Here are possible ways to incorporate a token economy system at school:

- Students can be paid (or given a token) for attendance. This payment can be in the form of real money or in the form of privileges. For example, someone with perfect attendance for a month might be allowed to skip study hall for a week.
- Students can be given tokens for grades. For example, people who make the "B" honor roll could be given free lunches for a week from the school cafeteria. (Students may groan that this is not a reward.)

These two suggestions are somewhat generic, but encourage students to tailor a token economy system to THEIR school. What kinds of behaviors should be rewarded? What kinds of rewards would motivate these behaviors? Emphasize creativity and you may get some wild suggestions.

4. *Despite the many problems associated with chemotherapy, why would it be virtually impossible and even undesirable for a mental institution to eliminate chemotherapy completely? What kinds of problems would result? Explain.*

As mentioned in the text, drugs given in moderation and careful supervision can be quite useful. Without these drugs, many patients would simply become unmanageable.

5. *Imagine that one of your parents was severely depressed for several months, that he or she has been completely listless and uncommunicative. All kinds of treatments have been ineffective. The last resort seems to be ECT; however, the hospital needs your approval to administer it. Do you give your approval? Why or why not? Explain.*

Answers will vary.

6. *Do you think it would ever be justified to use psychosurgery as punishment for criminals in prison? Why or why not? Explain.*

If you decide to discuss this question in class, use discretion. Students who believe that psychosurgery should be used as punishment may unintentionally appear cruel or sadistic. To avoid this, do NOT "debate" the question. Simply ask for "pros" and "cons" of using psychosurgery as punishment.

7. *Of all the therapies and treatments discussed in the chapter, which one would you tend to prefer if you had a problem? Explain.*

Answers will vary.

C) TEXTBOOK ACTIVITIES

1. If you do not have a mental health facility in your area, you and your class may want to compose a questionnaire or a letter that you can send to a state mental hospital.

2. Mention to students that if the therapists who are interviewed seem particularly excited about sharing their expertise, perhaps they can invite the therapists into class to speak.

3-4. These activities can be highly entertaining. However, be sure to follow up each role-playing situation or skit with a brief analysis. Was the dialogue essentially accurate? Was each therapist depicted accurately? Also, make it clear that despite the humor in some of the skits, intended or otherwise, real therapy is not something to laugh about. Moreover, we shouldn't ridicule or look down upon those who decide to consult a therapist. All of us, at one time or another, may need the help of a professional, and it requires courage to admit this.

5. This activity can be a rewarding one for students. However, before assigning it, review Rogers's nondirective technique. Otherwise, students may regard the exercise as a game and manipulate their friends into talking about their problems. The real purpose of the exercise is not to manipulate, but to support and demonstrate concern, which, in turn, will encourage the "troubled" person to open up.

6. This activity can easily be adapted and used for in-class journal writing. Simply have students keep track of their day-to-day negative internalized sentences for about a week and have them analyze these sentences.

D) IN-CLASS ACTIVITIES / LESSON SUGGESTIONS

1. See Chapter 7 of this manual, In-Class Acitivity #4, for ideas on how to incorporate a token economy system in your class.

2. Consider using textbook Discussion Question #3 in class. Break the class into small groups and have each think of a specific way to incorporate a token economy system at your school.

3. Before discussing Rogers's nondirective therapy, conduct a role-playing activity. One person should be given a hypothetical problem to talk about. For example, the person could talk about how his or her parents always fight, or about a dating relationship that is breaking up, and so on. Be sure that the problem is not a real one for the students involved. The other person should respond like he or she would normally do in such a situation. This will probably involve advice, questions, rebuttals, and so on. Then discuss the things that a listener should and should not do in such a situation. Is it okay to offer advice? Should the listener recount his or her own story about a similar problem?

    Finally, discuss Rogers's method of listening and contrast this with the "methods" discussed in class. Once students understand Rogers's ideas, role-play the same situation with the listener this time using Rogers's technique. The situation may seem less natural this time since everyone is aware of what is supposed to happen. In fact, even in a real situation, the listener may initially feel that simply mirroring responses is artificial, that it is a game. Point out, however, that if the listener sincerely cares about the other person, this artificiality will soon fade. Remember, the main purpose of mirroring responses is to SHOW the other person that you're listening and to provide a nonjudgmental atmosphere.

4. If you do not assign textbook Activities #3 and #4, consider conducting them in class. Break the class into small groups and have each group write a dialogue.

5. Find the nonemergency number of a mental health hotline in your area and assign one person to call and interview someone at the hotline. What kinds of techniques do they use to keep the person talking? What kinds of questions do they ask? What kinds of things do they absolutely avoid? Have your students report his or her findings to the class. Compare and contrast these findings to the therapies presented in the chapter. Which is most similar?

6. A final note about the chapter: The classroom is absolutely not the proper setting for therapy. Students should not be analyzed or probed simply to illustrate a method of therapy. For this reason, the number of activities you can perform in class becomes necessarily limited. You will just have to rely this time on your dazzling lecture skills.

20 Social Influences and Relationships

A. CHAPTER OUTLINE

■ HIDDEN INFLUENCES IN BEHAVIOR

■ ATTRIBUTION THEORY
    Antecedents
    Attribution
    Consequences

■ INTERPERSONAL ATTRACTION
    Importance of Associations
    Ingredients in Liking and Loving

■ AGGRESSION AND VIOLENCE
    Influence of the Brain
    Environment and Aggression
    Psychological Factors in Aggression
        Deindividuation
        Risky Shift Phenomenon

    Biological Factors in Aggression
    Effects of Mass Media
        Basic Film Studies
            Imitation Learning
        Trying for Perspective
            Field Studies
            Correlational Studies
    Catharsis

■ HELPING BEHAVIOR
    Diffusion of Responsibility
    Evaluation Apprehension

■ ENVIRONMENTAL INFLUENCES ON BEHAVIOR
    Density
    Crowding

B) TEXTBOOK DISCUSSION QUESTIONS

1. *A nonhuman but intelligent being captures you and explains that the only way it will set you free is if you adequately define the concept of love. Define it.*

   Definitions will vary. You'll probably receive some humorous answers.

2. *Some people argue that love is a subject that should not be scrutinizied under a microscope by psychologists. Do you tend to agree or disagree with this? Explain.*

   Accept any answers that are supported. Ask the following question to those students who believe that love should not be studied by psychologists: Do you also believe that love should not be "studied" or dis#ussed by philosophers, poets, novelists, journalists, and so on?

3. *Imagine a high school where there was a real possibility for violence on a daily basis. You can probably assume that a certain amount of deindividuation exists at the school. Give several possible reasons for this deindividuation. For example, you may say, "The school is probably very large." Then describe several ways in which you might decrease this deindividuation.*

   This is a good question to discuss in class. Possible reasons for deindividuation: a) The same few people always get blamed for the violence—which allows others to commit violence without being named; b) Witnesses to the violence fail to report it to avoid dangerous repercussions later; c) Teachers and administrators turn their backs to the violence because they feel that police work is not part of their job descriptions; or maybe they claim that they do not get paid enough to risk their lives.

4. *As made clear in the chapter, psychologists have accumulated a great deal of information about why people help or do not help others. What should we do now with this information in order to increase helping behavior in our society? Explain. Or do you believe that nothing can be done to increase helping behavior? Explain.*

   Answers will vary. One could argue that simply educating people about why people help or do not help will increase altruistic behavior.

5. *How might diffusion of responsibility occur within a typical family situation? Describe several examples.*

   A father might not pick up his dirty clothes off the floor if he suspects that someone else will do it. A mother may not vacuum the carpet if she believes that someone else will do it. A daughter may not change her baby sister's diapers because she does not feel it is her responsibility—she has several younger brothers and sisters who should do it. And so on.

6. *The chapter explains that evaluation apprehension during an emergency decreases the likelihood of someone helping. In what ways could evaluation apprehension help to create emergencies? Also, offer several real examples of emergencies perhaps caused by evaluation apprehension. For example, one could argue that those who saw problems with the space shuttle before it exploded did not voice their opinions loudly enough because of evaluation apprehension.*

Evaluation apprehension could create an emergency if someone suspects potential danger, but says nothing. For example, a construction worker may suspect that his or her foreman is drilling a hole near a gas pipe, but does not say anything because he or she fears that the suspicion MAY be silly and unfounded. One could argue that the following were caused, in part, by evaluation apprehension: Pearl Harbor, Cuban Missile Crisis, numerous terrorist acts.

7. *Describe a personal experience where density ws low but crowding was high, and describe an experience where density was high but crowding low. Be specific.*

Answers will vary.

C) TEXTBOOK ACTIVITIES

1. Before assigning this activity, be sure that students have a good grasp of attribution theory.

2. Mention to students that their photographs need to be somewhat uniform. For example, they should ALL be black-and-white or ALL color; none of the people in the photos should be wearing eyeglasses—or they ALL should be wearing them; ALL the photos should be portraits rather than candids; and so on.

3. By now, you may be tired of grading dry research papers. This activity should provide a welcome variation—for both you and your students. Consider using a similar format for other research activities listed throughout the text.

4-5. These are two more activities that force students to present their research in a creative fashion. Consider assigning half the class Activity #4 and the other half Activity #5. Then conduct an informal debate in class.

6. At this point in the course, students should be quite proficient at conducting experiments and analyzing data. However, they still may need to be reminded that they MUST fall in an identical way each time, that their appearance must remain constant for each trial, and so on. What varies and what remains constant, of course, will depend on the chosen hypothesis. As suggested in the text, be sure to approve the hypotheses; students can formulate some bizarre ideas.

7. Have student show you their data sheets BEFORE they conduct this activity. This will ensure that they're prepared to collect data.

The library experiment could easily be converted into a "bench experiment" at a park. One third of the time, an experimenter could sit at the end of a long bench, which would hypothetically encourage the greatest number of subjects to sit at the same bench. Another third of the time, an experimenter could sit in the middle, which would encourage the fewest number of subjects to sit on the same bench. During the final trials, an experimenter could sit between the middle and the end of the bench, which would encourage a moderate or average amount of subjects to sit at the same bench.

D) IN-CLASS ACTIVITIES / LESSON SUGGESTIONS

1. Use **MASTERS 20-2** and **20-3** to conduct textbook Activity #1 in class. Pass out one master to half the class and the other master to the other half.

2. With a little preparation, you could easily conduct textbook Activity #2 in class, also.

3. Spend a few minutes discussing popular definitions or descriptions of love: "Love is for the birds; love is a many splendord thing"; and so on. You can generate plenty of ideas by having them think of popular songs. Then tell students to write "Love _____" at the top of a sheet of paper. Allow them about five minutes to fill in the blank with as many "definitions" of love as possible. (You may want to break them into groups.) Encourage them to be creative and even humorous. You should receive some wacky answers. Collect all the papers and without revealing names, read the definitions. As you do this, YOU need to look beyond the wackiness of some of the answers and perhaps find a jewel of wisdom in them. You can accomplish this simply by asking questions. For example, let's say someone writes, "Love stinks." Rather than cackling and going on to the next definition, laugh, THEN ask, "In what way does love stink? Do you mean it causes pain? Is the pain worth it?" Of course, you don't want to overanalyze each answer, but you may get more out of some definitions than you might expect.

4. You may have several students who have had relatively long dating relationships. Perhaps these people would like to share their ideas on why or how liking turns to love. Students may feel uncomfortable using the word love in this context, but they probably will answer more general questions: "In what way did your relationship change as time went by? Do you worry sometimes about becoming too close to the other person? Does it require work to keep the relationship going? Does the relationship ever get boring?"

   Once you've exhausted discussion on this specific kind of love (and you may not—students enjoy talking about it), perhaps you can shift the discussion to other kinds of love—at home, with friends, and so on. How is this love similar? Different? Is it important to TELL family and friends that we love them? Or is SHOWING love enough?

5. Before students read about the reasons why people do not help in emergencies, tell them about the Kitty Genovese attack. Explain that since the incident, psychologists have been fascinated with finding reasons for the apparent apathy during emergencies. Then break them into small groups and have each group think of two possible hypotheses about why people do not help in emergencies and a way to test each hypothesis. This should demonstrate to them how difficult it is sometimes to think of hypotheses and to devise a plan to test them. If students do not get a chance to devise these plans, they MAY perceive the altruism experiments presented in the text as simple and uninspiring; and the conclusions may seem like common sense. If they DO get the chance to devise their own experiments, they'll probably realize how clever the actual experiments are.

6. You can probably conduct your own mini-experiment on helping behavior just outside your classroom. Assign about four students to be experimenters. Tell them that they can be a few minutes late to class for the next several days. Instead of rushing to class, they should drop their books several times on the way and measure who helps. These experimenters may need partners to record this data. Have the class decide on a hypothesis they want to test. Perhaps two experimenters could drop books in a more secluded hallway; the other two could drop books in a crowded one. Or two experimenters could complain after dropping the books and the other two could remain silent. Whatever hypothesis is chosen, make sure that ALL experimenters drop their books in the same manner each time. Practice in class! And if you're not testing for gender differences, the experimenters should probably all be the same sex.

21 Attitudes and Beliefs

A. CHAPTER OUTLINE

■ ATTITUDES
   Reference Groups
   Fitting Attitudes to the Group
      Prisoner-Guard Experiment

■ HOW WE VIEW OTHERS
   Stereotypes
   Prejudice
      Illusory Correlations
      Overcoming Prejudice
   Scapegoats
   Removing Deviates

■ CHANGING ATTITUDES
   Cognitive Dissonance
   Yielding to Others
   Compliance with Authority
      Stanley Milgram

■ VERBAL PERSUASION
   Defenses Against Persuasion
      Immunization
   Effect of Having an Expert

■ SOCIAL PERSUASION: THE POLYGRAPH
   Social Basis of Lie Detector
   Accuracy of Polygraph

■ SOCIAL PERSUASION: BRAINWASHING
   Friendliness
   Sensory Deprivation
   Reward System
   Brainwashing and the Consumer

B) TEXTBOOK DISCUSSION QUESTIONS

1-4. 1. *Describe two of your most important reference groups. Discuss several similarities and differences between these two groups. Overall, are there more similarities or differences? Explain.*

2. *List several stereotypes of teachers and discuss (without using names) whether your teachers this year fit these stereotypes.*

3. *If you were dating someone for several months and then found out that this person was extremely prejudiced against a certain ethnic group, do you think you might eventually stop dating this person for this reason? Yes? No? Depends? Explain.*

4. *Compare some of the attitudes you have today with those you had when you were in junior high school. Have they remained basically the same? If yes, do you express them differently? Explain.*

Answers will vary. These questions, especially #3, should inspire lively in-class discussions.

5. *While Milgram's obedience studies are fascinating, they also put the subjects involved under a great deal of stress at times. Experimenters always need to strike a balance between how they get their results and what they find out. Some might argue that Milgram's studies do not achieve this balance, that it is not ethical to put subjects under this great stress, regardless of what is learned. Do you agree? Why or why not? Explain.*

To discuss this question in class, write two lists on the board. "List A" should include WHAT Milgram learned through his studies. "List B" should include HOW Milgram performed his studies and any drawbacks that this involved. Actually, just write the headings for the two lists and have students fill them in with their own ideas.

6. *How do advertisers establish credibility for their products? Describe several real advertising examples to support your answer.*

Advertisers establish credibility by showing "doctors" promoting aspirin, physically fit people eating healthy foods, attractive people using beauty products, and so on.

7. *As noted in the chapter, sensory deprivation may cause hallucinations. What kinds of workers or managers would definitely need to know this information? Explain. Keep in mind that not all the senses need to be deprived at one time to cause problems.*

The following are workers who may be affected by sensory deprivation: truck drivers, air traffic controllers, factory workers on an assembly line, security guards, English teachers who must listen to ninety-three speeches in a row.

8. *One of the suggestions listed at the end of the chapter was to write a list of job skills that you have developed. You may not have an interview soon, but this will be good practice. So, go ahead and write down your skills now.*

"Skills" will vary!

C) TEXTBOOK ACTIVITIES

1. You may want to give students the option of NOT allowing you to read their letters. Perhaps they can simply show them to you to prove that they wrote them.

2. See In-Class Activity #3 below.

3. Students should have no difficulty finding information on this topic. Consider inviting a police officer to class to speak about cults.

4. Students should have fun with this one.

5-6. These last two activities, like many of the others in this text, force students to become actively involved in the learning process. They can't simply sit back and copy information from an encyclopedia. Keep in mind, however, that this higher involvement, while beneficial and more fun than writing a typical research report, requires an extra or, at least, a different kind of effort from students. Because of this, students may need extra encouragement and direction from you.

D) IN-CLASS ACTIVITIES / LESSON SUGGESTIONS

1. To demonstrate how reference groups affect attitudes, write three or four categories on the board, one at a time, and have students make a list of their attitudes toward these categories. For example, if you write, "Republican," they might write, "Concerned with America's future, conservative, I'd prefer to vote for a Republican," and so on. Have them conduct this same activity on their parents that night, and then have them compare and contrast the two lists.

    The attitudes will probably be highly similar, which should demonstrate that parents constitute for most of us—at least during adolescence—an important reference group.

    Here are some categories you can write on the board to "measure" attitudes: Catholics, welfare, alcohol, college, money, books, school, animals.

    You might want to try a variation of this activity. Have students compare their lists this time with a best friend to see if friends also constitute for them an important reference group. In this case, students may argue that they choose their friends because of similar interests, and not the other way around, This, of course, is partially true. Agree with them. But will THEY agree that their friends sometimes influence their attitudes? Maybe not. Don't their friends—even their peers—influence the kind of clothes they wear (have them look around the room)? Their hairstyles? Their language? Their attitudes toward school?

2. Discussion question #2 asks students to list several stereotypes of teachers. To illustrate the concept of stereotypes in class, ask the same question, but use additional labels: kindergarten teacher, nerd, old person, pizza delivery person, and so on. At times, there may be more than one label to describe a single group. For example, "cop" and "police officer" both refer to the same occupation, but one label might evoke different stereotypes than the other. Try it: one class can describe "cop"; the other can describe "police officer." Afterward, discuss whether most of the stereotypes listed for all the labels were primarily positive or negative.

3. The following is an adaptation of textbook Activity #2. Read each of the following word pairs below slowly—once only. Students should sit back and pay attention. Do not give them any other instructions. Afterwards pass out **MASTER 21-2** (Memory Test) and have students record the number of times they believe the word pair was read.

    Note that two word pairs on **MASTER 21-2** (#3, milk-tea, and #7, cricket-stocking) will not be read by you at all. These are included to make it appear that the frequency of the word pairs varies. Otherwise, students may simply write down "5" for all their answers, assuming that the frequency is uniform. Also, there are two word pairs on the long list below (#5, dirt-wood, and #10, football-field) that you will read very frequently. These are included for the same reason. If this sounds confusing, all you have to remember is that when analyzing your data, you will ignore #3, #5, #7, and #10. The following are word pairs that you will analyze. FAMILIAR word pairs: #1, #4, #8, #11, #13. UNFAMILIAR word pairs: #2, #6, #9, #12, #14.

    Once students have filled out **MASTER 21-2**, hand out **MASTER 21-3**. This is a data sheet that will help you and your students organize and analyze your data. Note that each of the familiar word pairs below will be read five times and each of the unfamiliar word pairs will also be read five times. If "Total A" on the data sheet then is higher than "Total B," you can probably conclude that illusory correlations contributed to this.

Once students complete their data sheets, you can tally and average everyone's totals to see if the class as a whole formed illusory correlations. (You can even compare answers to #5, the high frequency, unfamiliar word pair, to answers to #10, the high frequency, familiar word pair.)

WORD-PAIRS

cat-meow	dirt-wood
table-coat	cat-meow
fork-spoon	wallet-ankle
dirt-wood	football-field
football-field	fork-spoon
wallet-ankle	gamble-bed
brick-house	dirt-wood
gamble-bed	football-field
dirt-wood	brick-house
football-field	tree-carpet
bacon-eggs	bacon-eggs
tree-carpet	table-coat
wing-bird	wing-bird
money-toilet	money-toilet
wallet-ankle	fork-spoon
brick-house	dirt-wood
gamble-bed	gamble-bed
dirt-wood	football-field
bacon-eggs	wallet-ankle
football-field	cat-meow
tree-carpet	brick-house
wing-bird	dirt-wood
cat-meow	table-coat
table-coat	wing-bird
dirt-wood	money-toilet
money-toilet	football-field
football-field	bacon-eggs
fork-spoon	tree-carpet
tree-carpet	
wing-bird	
cat-meow	
table-coat	
dirt-wood	
wallet-ankle	
football-field	
brick-house	
gamble-bed	
money-toilet	
dirt-wood	
fork-spoon	
bacon-eggs	
football-field	

4. The text describes how Nazis used Jews as scapegoats. Do certain groups today still use scapegoats? To find out, have students look through the newspaper for several days and pick out possible examples.

5. The chapter explains that most people blindly obey authority because they are not given full responsibility for their own actions. This can be easily demonstrated in class. Without explanation, order a student to bring a notebook to your desk. Order another student to bring something from his or her pocket. Order another to take off his or her shoes. And so on. The orders should become progressively more outlandish — but don't go too far! Most students will readily comply since they probably believe that what happens in your class, under your orders, is YOUR responsibility. Even after explaining your point about blind obedience and responsibility, some students will continue to comply if you demand something.

   One technique that will nearly guarantee obedience is your use of distance. If you ask someone from across the room to take off a shoe, the person MAY not do it. Stand face-to-face with the same person, and the rate of obedience soars. Try it and discuss whether it seemed to work. (This same technique works well with students who disrupt class. Instead of reprimanding these students, simply walk close to them and continue teaching.)

6. The end of the chapter describes how consumers are often "brainwashed." If you've ever bought a new car, you're familiar with the salesperson's masterful "brainwashing" techniques, where small requests are followed by a reward and then by large requests: "If you did buy a car from us, what color would you like? Sharp color. Would you get just a radio or a tape player as well?" And so on. If you're familiar with these techniques, share them with the class.

   Many of your students may work for retailers or spend a great deal of time shopping at stores whose employees also use these techniques. If so, they can probably think of numerous examples.

7. Here's a final role-playing exercise in which YOU should probably participate. Make up a clever name for a company—your company—and interview several students for an important job opening. Afterward, have students point out the positive and negative aspects about each student's responses. Next, discuss the job interview techniques outlined at the end of the chapter. Finally, interview several more students, and this time students should consciously try to incorporate some of these techniques during the "interview."

Section
2

**Sources for
Background Materials and Audiovisual Materials**

■ BACKGROUND MATERIALS

Bunker, Barbara Benedict. A STUDENT'S GUIDE TO CONDUCTING SOCIAL SCIENCE RESEARCH. New York: Human Sciences Press, Inc. 1975.

Kimble, G.A. and K. Schlesinger. TOPICS IN THE HISTORY OF PSYCHOLOGY. (2 volumes). N.Y.: Lawrence Erlbaum, 1985.

Smith, Samuel. IDEAS OF THE GREAT PSYCHOLOGISTS. New York: Harper and Row, 1983.

■ AUDIOVISUAL MATERIALS *

INTRODUCTION TO PSYCHOLOGY. Filmstrip (4 parts). Educational Audio Visuals. Pleasantville, N.Y. 10570.

LANDMARKS IN PSYCHOLOGY. Filmstrip (3 parts). Human Relations Media. Pleasantville, N. Y. 10570.

All audiovisual materials are 16 mm and color unless otherwise indicated.

UNIT 2: BIOLOGICAL INFLUENCES (CHAPTERS 3-6)

■ BACKGROUND MATERIALS

Asimov, Isaac. THE HUMAN BRAIN: ITS CAPACITIES AND FUNCTIONS. N.Y.: Signet.

Brandes, Louis Grant. AN INTRODUCTION TO OPTICAL ILLUSIONS. J. Weston Walch Publisher, P.O. Box 658, Portland, Maine 04104-0658 (32 posters).

Rainer, Tristine. THE NEW DIARY. N.Y. : St. Martin's Press, 1978.

Restak, Richard. M.D.   THE BRAIN (COMPANION TO PBS TELEVISION SERIES). N.Y.: Bantam, 1987.
— THE MIND. N.Y.: Bantam, 1988

Seymour, Dale. VISUAL THINKING. Dale Seymour Publications, P.O. Box 10888, Palo Alto, CA 94303   (Flash cards that test visual thinking skills).

Springer, Sally P. and George Deutsch. LEFT BRAIN, RIGHT BRAIN. N.Y.: W.H. Freeman, 1985.

STATES OF CONSCIOUSNESS. N.Y. : The American Psychological Association, 1981.

Ullman, Montague, M.D. and Nan Zimmerman. WORKING WITH DREAMS. N.Y. : St. Martin's Press, 1979.

Wonder, Jacquelyn and Priscilla Donovan. WHOLE BRAIN THINKING. N.Y. : Willian Morrow and Co., 1984.

■ AUDIOVISUAL MATERIALS

BASIC PSYCHOLOGY: PERCEPTION, 16 min, 1973.

BIOFEEDBACK: THE YOGA OF THE WEST, 38 min, 1974.

THE HIDDEN UNIVERSE: THE BRAIN, 50 min, 1977.

MIRACLE OF THE MIND, 25 min, 1967.

PERCEPTION, 29 min, 1979.

THEATRE OF THE NIGHT: THE SCIENCE OF SLEEP AND DREAMS. (Filmstrip)

■ BACKGROUND MATERIALS

Skinner, B. F. BEYOND FREEDOM AND DIGNITY. N.Y. : Bantam, 1971.

Von Oech, Roger, Ph.D. A WHACK ON THE SIDE OF YOUR HEAD: HOW TO UNLOCK YOUR MIND FOR INNOVATION. N.Y. : Warner Books, 1983.

■ AUDIOVISUAL MATERIALS

THE POWER OF POSITIVE REINFORCEMENT, 28 min, 1978.

B.F. SKINNER: LEARNING THROUGH REWARDS. (Filmstrip)

UNIT 4: HUMAN DEVELOPMENT (CHAPTERS 10-13)

■ BACKGROUND MATERIALS

Bender, David L. ed. PROBLEMS OF DEATH: OPPOSING VIEWPOINTS.
St. Paul: Greenhaven Press, 1981.

Dilley, Josiah. ...AND I THOUGHT I KNEW HOW TO COMMUNICATE: FRESH CHOICES
IN RELATING. Minneapolis: Educational Media Corp. 1985.

Elkind, David. ALL GROWN UP AND NO PLACE TO GO. Reading: Addison- Wesley Publ.,
1984.

Galbraith, Ronald E. and Thomas M. Jones. MORAL REASONING.Greenhaven Press.
1976.

Kubler-Ross, Elisabeth. ON DEATH AND DYING. N.Y. : MacMillan, 1969.

Lee, James L., Ph.D. and Charles J. Pulvino, Ph.D. WHO AM I: SELF EXPLORATION SERIES.
Media Corp., Box 21311, Minneapolis, MN 55421 (computer disks).

Mills, Gretchen. et al. DISCUSSING DEATH: A GUIDE TO DEATH EDUCATION. Palm
Spring: ETC Publ., 1976.

Pogrebin, Letty Cottin. AMONG FRIENDS. N.Y. : McGraw-Hill. 1987.

■ AUDIOVISUAL MATERIALS

AGING, 21 min, 1973.

ANXIETY AND YOUNG ADULTS: PSYCHOLOGICAL PROBLEMS OF YOUTH. (Filmstrip)

EVERYBODY RIDES THE CAROUSEL, Parts 1-3, 24, 21, and 29 min, 1975.

IN SEARCH OF LIFE AFTER DEATH, 24 min, 1976.

MORAL DEVELOPMENT, 28 min, 1973.

RAISED IN ANGER: A SPECIAL PROGRAM ON CHILD ABUSE, 59 min (2 reels), 1979.

ROCK-A-BYE-BABY. 29 min, 1971.

TEENAGE TROUBLES: HOW TO SURVIVE THE TEENAGE YEARS. (Filmstrip)

UNIT 5: PERSONALITY AND ADJUSTMENT (CHAPTERS 14-17)

■ BACKGROUND MATERIALS

Burns, David D. FEELING GOOD: THE NEW MOOD THERAPY. N.Y. : Signet, 1980.

Fromm, Erich. THE ART OF LOVING. N.Y. : Harper and Row, 1956.

Hall, Calvin S. A PRIMER OF FREUDIAN PSYCHOLOGY. N.Y. : Signet,1954.

Houston, Jean. THE POSSIBLE HUMAN: A COURSE IN ENHANCING YOUR PHYSICAL, MENTAL, AND CREATIVE ABILITIES.   N.Y. : St. Martin's Press, 1982.

James, Muriel and Dorothy Jongeward. BORN TO WIN: TRANSACTIONAL ANALYSIS WITH GESTALT EXPERIMENTS. Reading: AddisonWesley Publ., 1973.

Lager, Marilyn. SIGMUND FREUD: DOCTOR OF THE MIND. New Jersey: Enslow Publ.

Lair, Jess. I AIN'T WELL, BUT I SURE AM BETTER. Greenwich: Fawcett, 1975.

Powell, John. WHY AM I AFRAID TO TELL YOU WHO I AM? Niles: Argus Communications, 1969.

Stafford-Clark, David. WHAT FREUD REALLY SAID. N.Y.: Shocken Books, 1966.

Stevens, John 0. AWARENESS: EXPLORING, EXPERIMENTING, EXPERIENCING. N.Y. : Bantam, 1971.

■ AUDIOVISUAL MATERIALS

EVALUATING PERSONALITY: FROM INKBLOTS TO INTUITION. (Filmstrip)

MENTAL WELLNESS: MAKING IT HAPPEN. (Video)

STUDENT STRESS: COPING WITH ACADEMIC PRESSURES. (Video)

SUICIDE: A TEENAGE DILEMMA. (Video)

WINNING ISN'T EVERYTHING?, 23 min, 1978.

UNIT 6: ABNORMAL PSYCHOLOGY (CHAPTERS 18-19)

■ BACKGROUND MATERIALS

Axline, Virginia M. DIBS IN SEARCH OF SELF. N.Y. : Ballantine, 1964.

Greenberg, Joanne. I NEVER PROMISED YOU A ROSE GARDEN. N.Y. : Signet, 1964.

Keyes, Daniel. FLOWERS FOR ALGERNON. N.Y.: Bantam, 1968.

Kesey, Ken. ONE FLEW OVER THE CUCKOO'S NEST. N.Y.: Viking, 1962.

Sechehaye, Marguerite. AUTOBIOGRAPHY OF A SCHIZOPHRENIC GIRL. N.Y.: New American Library, 1951.

Torrey, E. Fuller. NOWHERE TO GO: THE TRAGIC ODYSSEY OF THE HOMELESS MENTALLY ILL, 1989.

■ AUDIOVISUAL MATERIALS

ABNORMAL BEHAVIOR: A MENTAL HOSPITAL, 28 min, 1977.

ATTACKING ANXIETY. (Video)

BLAHS, BLUES, AND BETTER DAYS, 19 min, 1973.

A BOY NAMED TERRY EGAN, 52 min (2 reels), 1973.

PERSONALITY DISORDERS: FAILURES OF ADJUSTMENT. (Filmstrip)

PSYCHOLOGICAL DEFENSES. (Filmstrip)

UNIT 7: SELF AND SOCIETY (CHAPTERS 20-21)

■ BACKGROUND MATERIALS

Alberti, Robert E., Ph.D. and Michael L. Emmons, Ph.D. YOUR PERFECT RIGHT: A GUIDE
TO ASSERTIVE LIVING. San Luis Obispo: Impact Publ., 1984.

Eysenck, H.M. MINDWATCHING: WHY PEOPLE BEHAVE THE WAY THEY DO.
N.Y.: Anchor / Doubleday, 1983.

■ AUDIOVISUAL MATERIALS

EXPERIMENTS IN HUMAN BEHAVIOR. (Filmstrip)

GROUPTHINK, 22 min, 1973.

WHEN WILL PEOPLE HELP: BYSTANDER INTERVENTION, 25 min, 1976.

GENERAL BACKGROUND MATERIALS

ANNUAL EDITIONS SERIES (PSYCHOLOGY, HUMAN DEVELOPMENT, ETC.).
Dushkin Publ. Group, Sluice Dock, Guilford, Conn. 06437.

Benjamin, Ludy T. and Kathleen D. Lowman, Eds. ACTIVITES HANDBOOK
FOR THE TEACHING OF PSYCHOLOGY.
Washington: American Psychological Association, 1981.

INTRODUCTORY PSYCHOLOGY THROUGH SCIENCE FICTION. Chicago: Rand, 1974.

Kehayan, V. Alex. SAGE: SELF-AWARENESS GROWTH EXPERIENCES, GRADES
7-12. Rolling Hills Estates: B.L. Winch and Assoc., 1983.

Progoff, Ira. AT A JOURNAL WORKSHOP. N.Y.: Dialogue House Library, 1975.

Rubinstein, Joseph and Brent Slife. TAKING SIDES: CLASHING VIEWS ON
CONTROVERSIAL PSYCHOLOGICAL ISSUES. Guilford: Dushkin
Publ. Group, 1986.

Simon, Sidney, et. al. VALUES CLARIFICATION. N.Y. : A and W Visual Library, 1972.

Smuin, Stephen K. TURN-ONS: 185 STRATEGIES FOR THE SECONDARY

CLASSROOM. Belmont: Fearon Pitman Publ., 1978.

**WHERE TO ORDER MANY OF THE BACKGROUND MATERIALS LISTED
THROUGHOUT THIS SECTION:**

SOCIAL STUDIES SCHOOL SERVICE
10200 JEFFERSON BOULEVARD, ROOM 3
P.O. BOX 802
CULVER CITY, CA 90232-0802

**WHERE TO ORDER MANY OF THE FILMSTRIPS AND VIDEOS LISTED
THROUGHOUT THIS SECTION**

HUMAN RELATIONS MEDIA
175 TOMPKINS AVENUE
PLEASANTVILLE, NY 10570

Section 3

Masters

Master 1-1

CHAPTER ONE LEARNING GOALS

1. What is the definition of psychology?

2. What are the main differences between research and applied psychologists?

3. What is the role of reason in philosophy?

4. How did Socrates, Plato, and Aristotle contribute to our understanding of behavior?

5. How does astrology work and how reliable is it?

6. When did the period called the dark ages occur? Why was it called the dark ages?

7. When did the period called the middle ages occur? Why was it called the middle ages?

8. What does "renaissance" mean? When did the Renaissance occur? What discoveries were made during this period?

9. When was Charles Darwin's theory first published? Why was the theory important?

10. Who is considered the father of psychology? Why is 1879 important?

11. What is introspection? What are some limitations of introspection?

12. What is eclecticism?

13. What are the main beliefs of the following five approaches to studying human nature: neurobiological, behavioral, humanistic, psychoanalytical, cognitive?

14. What does SQ3R stand for? What is it used for?

15. What are eight occupational possibilities for psychologists?

Master 1-2

FIVE APPROACHES TO STUDYING BEHAVIOR

TEXTBOOK DISCUSSION QUESTION #6 (CHAPTER 1)

Maria wants to ask for a raise, but begins to sweat uncontrollably every time she even gets near her boss. Using the five approaches described in the chapter, briefly describe how each might explain this simple behavior.

NEUROBIOLOGICAL APPROACH:

"Maria has little control over how her body reacts in this situation. She was probably involved in a similar situation in the past that caused an extreme reaction. Also, we need to examine other physiological reactions that Maria experiences—not just the sweating."

BEHAVIORAL APPROACH:

"Maria has little choice in this or any other situation. The environment has actually caused her to sweat. If the boss, or some other authority figures, had rewarded her in the past, she would now have no difficulty approaching her boss."

HUMANISTIC APPROACH:

"Maria is potentially a good person, but she doesn't seem to realize that completely in this situation. With some encouragement from her boss, she might realize this inner strength she already possesses.

PSYCHOANALYTICAL APPROACH:

"Maria's uneasiness with her boss probably represents some hidden anxiety toward someone else in her past, someone probably very close to her. Through psychoanalysis, we might be able to find the original cause of her anxiety."

COGNITIVE APPROACH:

"Maria is probably telling herself that she is inferior and that she doesn't deserve a raise. If she can replace these statements with more realistic statements. she will feel better.

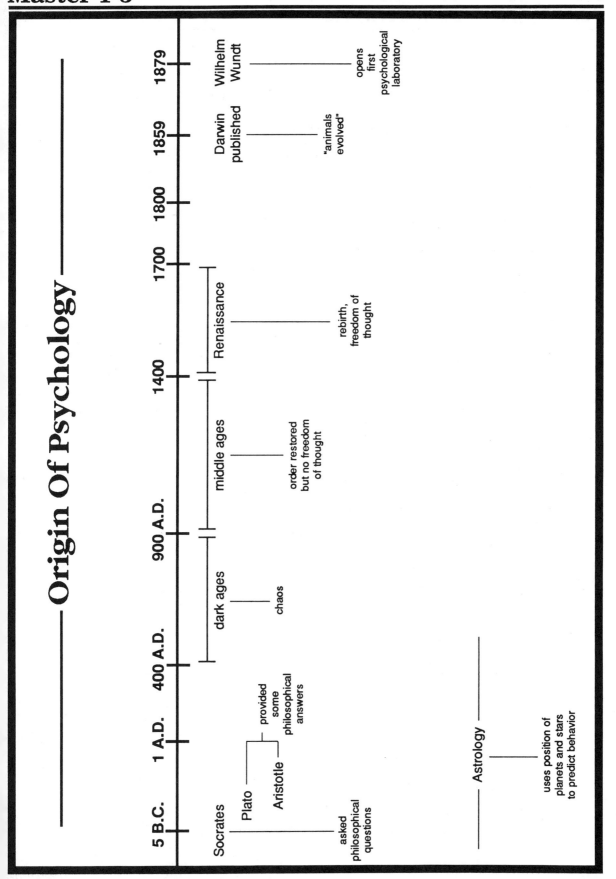

Origin Of Psychology

5 B.C. | 1 A.D. | 400 A.D. | 900 A.D. | 1400 | 1700 | 1800 | 1859 | 1879

Socrates

Plato

Aristotle

provided some philosophical answers

asked philosophical questions

dark ages

chaos

middle ages

order restored but no freedom of thought

Renaissance

rebirth, freedom of thought

Darwin published

"animals evolved"

Wilhelm Wundt

opens first psychological laboratory

Astrology

uses position of planets and stars to predict behavior

Master 2-1

CHAPTER 2 LEARNING GOALS

1. What is a placebo? Why is it used? What effect does it have on the body?

2. What is a hypothesis? On whom do researchers conduct their experiments?

3. Why is it important to guard against hidden or unexpected variables?

4. What's the difference between a dependent variable and an independent variable?

5. What are field experiments?

6. What is the difference between an experimental group and a control group?

7. What are the advantages and disadvantages in using the following methods for studying behavior:

> survey method
> naturalistic observation
> interviews
> case-study method
> psychological tests
> longitudinal studies
> cross sectional studies

8. What are four ethical principles for experimentation established by the American Psychological Association?

9. What are several criticisms of using animals in experiments?

10. Which gender seems to demonstrate better spatial ability? Why?

Master 2-2

EXPERIMENT GUIDELINE

Use the following guideline to summarize any experiments that you choose to conduct during the year. When you write up your report, include the label for each section. Actually write out "hypothesis," and so on.

TITLE: This should reveal the nature of your experiment.

HYPOTHESIS: This, of course, is your educated guess: you will try to prove or disprove it. Be sure to objectively define all the terms of your hypothesis. For example, if the term "permissive parents" was included, you would need to define this. Once you have formulated a hypothesis, don't change it just because your results are disproving it. It doesn't matter if your guess is right or wrong.

METHOD

    SUBJECTS: Your subjects are the people (or animals) that you test in your experiment. Added together, your subjects are called your "sample." In order for your results to be meaningful, your sample should be fairly large.

    List in this section as much of the following information as possible:
- a) exact number of subjects;
- b) approximate ages:
- c) sex of subjects:
- d) how subjects were chosen (for almost all experiments, subjects should be chosen randomly);
- e) where subjects were found (which mall? Which high school? etc.);
- f) if subjects were alone or in a group when approached:
- g) how many subjects were in experimental group & how many were in control group (control group includes those not exposed to independent variable). The number of subjects in the experimental and control groups should be equal (unless there are unique problems or circumstances).

    APPARATUS: List everything that was used:
- a) equipment
- b) data sheets:
- c) surveys:
- d) a building.

    PROCEDURE: Explain EXACTLY how the experiment was conducted. Be specific: be objective: be precise. Don't leave out ANYTHING. Attach completed data sheets at the end of the report.

RESULTS: Analyze all data sheets and make as many computations as possible: percentages. averages. etc. Explain—IN WORDS—these results. Also, include a TABLE or CHART. similar to something you might find in PSYCHOLOGY TODAY or TIME or NEWSWEEK. Make the chart simple to read: use colors, underline. etc. The table or chart should SUMMARIZE all your data: it shouldn't simply be a replication of all your data sheets.

DISCUSSION: This is where you analyze and discuss your results. Address the following questions: Did the results support the hypothesis? Can any conclusions be drawn? How much confidence do you place in your results? What are some strengths and weaknesses of your experiment? What revisions would you make if you had to do the experiment over again? Can you generalize your findings to the rest of the population? Most importantly, discuss WHY you got the results you got. For example, WHY are people in sports cars less likely to stop at stop signs? Are they lazy? Are they trying to be cool? Are they ignorant? DISCUSS.

BIBLIOGRAPHY: Include any sources you may have used.

EXPERIMENTAL PROCEDURE

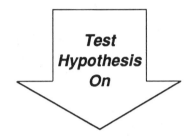

HYPOTHESIS

**If A (the independent variable) is presented or changed...
then B (the independent variable) will occur or change.**

**Test
Hypothesis
On**

SUBJECTS

*randomly
divide*

Into   *Into*

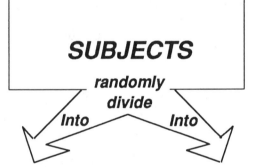

| *EXPERIMENTAL GROUP* (exposed to independent variable) | *CONTROL GROUP* (not exposed to independent variable) |

| *MEASURE BEHAVIOR* (the dependent variable) | *MEASURE BEHAVIOR* (the dependent variable) |

   *compare
measurements*

Master 3-1

LEARNING GOALS

1. The cerebral cortex is made up of two hemispheres. Which hemisphere controls the movements of the right side of the body? Which hemisphere controls the movements of the left side of the body?

2. What are the functions of the sensory and motor strips?

3. What part of the brain interprets what we see?

4. What are several functions of the frontal association area? What does the size of the frontal area usually reveal?

5. What does it mean to be dominant in one hemisphere?

6. What is the function of the corpus callosum? Where is it specifically located?

7. In what tasks do the left and right hemispheres specialize (for most people)?

8. What is the main difference between the cerebral cortex and the lower brain?

9. What are the four main parts of the lower brain? What are the functions of each part?

10. What is a neuron? What are the functions of axons and dendrites?

11. What is the relationship between a synapse and a neurotransmitter?

12. What is the specific function of acetycholine?

13. What is the relationship between nerve impulses of the body and the spinal cord?

14. What is the relationship between the spinal cord and reflexes?

15. What is the difference between the nervous system and the glandular or endocrine system?

16. What are hormones? When a hormone is release, what effect does this have on the body? Into what are hormones released? Where are hormones held before being released?

17. What are the functions of the pituitary, thyroid, and adrenal glands?

18. What are gonads? What is the difference between androgen and androgen?

Master 3-2

Fill in the blanks to form complete words or phrases. Some of the completed words may be proper nouns.

1. S T __ T __ __   __ __   __ __ B __ R T __

2. T __ __ N S __ __ __ T __ T __ __ N

3. S __ __ __ R __ A N

4. __ N D   N __ __   __   __ __ R D   __ R __ M
   __ __ R   S __ __ N S __ R S

5. __ O   N O __   __ N __ __ R

6. F __ __ T __ __ L L   F __ __ L __

7. __ __ R S __   __ L __ S S   __ __ __ L

8. T __ __   T __ __ __   T __ __ C T   __ __   __ __ W

9. __ H __ __ K S __ I V I __ __

10. __ L __ __ S __   D __   N __ __   __ __ __ D   T __ __
    __ N __ __ __ L S

HEMISPHERE DOMINANCE INVENTORY

Answer ALL of the following questions as quickly as possible. Do not skip any. If more than one answer applies, choose the one that best applies to you.

_____ 1. If you had to give someone directions to your house, which of the following methods would you most likely use?
   a) Write a paragraph that explains where and when to turn.
   b) Draw a road map.

_____ 2. Which of the following are you better at solving?
   a) Jigsaw puzzle
   b) Crossword puzzle

_____ 3. Do you remember faces easily?
   a) No
   b) Yes

_____ 4. Do you think you'd earn higher grades in a geometry class or in an algebra class?
   a) Geometry
   b) Algebra

_____ 5. Imagine that you're vacationing at a resort. Which of the following would you most likely do?
   a) Obtain a brochure of local attractions and plan what you'd like to do for the day.
   b) Drive around without a plan and decide what you'd like to do as you drive along.

_____ 6. Was it usually easy or difficult for you to learn grammar in school?
   a) Difficult
   b) Easy

_____ 7. Imagine enrolling in a music course. You and a partner in the course must write a song. Which of the following would you prefer to do? (Assume you have the ability to do both.)
   a) Write the lyrics.
   b) Compose the melody.

_____ 8. When you read a new chapter in a textbook, which of the following are you most likely to do?
   a) Skim through the entire chapter first to get a general idea of what the chapter is about.
   b) Read the chapter from beginning to end without doing much skimming.

_____ 9. In which of the following English classes would you most likely enroll?
   a) Journalism
   b) Creative writing

_____ 10. Imagine that you volunteered to work for the school newspaper. Which of the following would you rather do?
   a) Cut and paste and lay out the stories and decide which stories should appear where.
   b) Write one or two of the stories.

_____ 11. After reading a new chapter in a textbook, which of the following would you rather do?
   a) Summarize the chapter.
   b) Outline the chapter.

_____ 12. If you had an important project due in a class, would you rather work in a group or alone?
   a) Group
   b) Alone

_____ 13. Which of the following classroom situations do you prefer?
  a) A teacher announces assignments on a weekly basis and sets specific, weekly due dates.
  b) A teacher announces all the assignments at the beginning of the course and allows you to complete them at any time before the end of the course.
_____ 14. Which of the following statements best applies to you?
  a) I'm good at guessing a person's mood by his or her body language.
  b) I'm not good at guessing a person's mood by his or her body language.
_____ 15. Which of the following would you rather play?
  a) Scrabble
  b) Checkers
_____ 16. With which of the following statements do you most agree?
  a) We should continue exploring outer space since one day this exploration may benefit us.
  b) We should continue exploring outer space only if we can be sure ahead of time of certain benefits we would receive.

KEY

How many "a" answers did you have for odd-numbered questions?   _____

How many "b" answers did you have for even-numbered questions?   _____

Add up these two sums and this is your LEFT-HEMISPHERE total:

                                                                   _____

How many "a" answers did you have for even-numbered questions?   _____

How many "b" answers did you have for odd-numbered questions?   _____

Add up these two sums and this is your RIGHT-HEMISPHERE total: _____

Master 3-6

HEMISPHERE DOMINANCE INVENTORY FOR MOTOR SKILLS

For each of the following, answer LEFT, RIGHT, or BOTH.

1. With which hand do you write?

2. With which hand do you throw a ball?

3. Which hand do you use to hold scissors?

4. With which hand would you hammer a nail?

5. When holding a baseball bat, which hand is on top?

6. Which hand do you use to deal out playing cards?

7. When you fold your hands, which hand is on top?

8. When you cross your arms, which arm is usually on top?

9. When you cross your legs, which leg is usually on top?

10. With which foot do you kick a ball?

11. When putting on a pair a pants, which leg goes into the pants first?

12. If both your left and right shoes were lying together, which would you put on first?

13. When putting on a jacket or sweater, which arm goes into the sleeves first?

Master 4-1

CHAPTER 4 LEARNING GOALS

1. What is the difference between sensation and perception?

2. What is white light? What is the difference between infrared and ultraviolet wavelengths?

3. What are the functions of the following parts of the eye:

    cornea
    iris
    lens
    pupil
    retina

4. What is a blind spot?

5. What is the difference in function of a rod and a cone? Which of these shuts off at night?

6. What three colors make up color vision?

7. What does it mean to be mildly color blind (the common form of color blindness)? What does it mean to be completely color blind?

8. Why do afterimages occur?

9. What is the difference between pitch, intensity, and decibels?

10. What are the functions of the following parts of the ear: eardrum; cochlea; hair calls; auditory nerve?

11. What are the three types of skin receptors?

12. What are the functions of cilia and olfactory bulbs?

13. How do animals use smell to communicate sexual interest?

14. What four types of taste receptors do humans have? How do salt needs change as one grows older?

15. What are 4 perceptual constancies? How does each constancy affect perception?

16. What does the visual cliff experiment demonstrate?

17. How do binocular disparity and visual texture help in depth perception?

18. What is the difference between similarity and closure?

19. What is an illusion? Why does the Muller-Lyer illusion fool us?

20. What is a reversible figure?

21. What is subliminal perception?

22. What are 4 types of ESP commonly studied? What are the definitions of each type?

Master 4-2

PERCEPTUAL SET

Here's an activity to demonstrate how expectations influence perception.

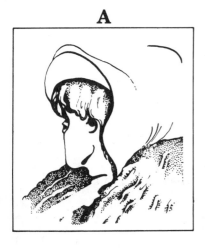

A

B

C

Show the pictures above in the following manner to two subjects. Show the first subject only picture A (cover up pictures B & C). Show the second subject only picture B. Once you're done, show both of them only picture C and ask what they see. The subject who saw A first, which is predominantly an older woman, will probably argue that C is an older woman. The friend who saw B first, which is predominantly a younger woman, will probably argue that C is a younger woman. In other words, they will perceive C differently because of their expectations. After looking at C for a while they should see both the younger and older woman.

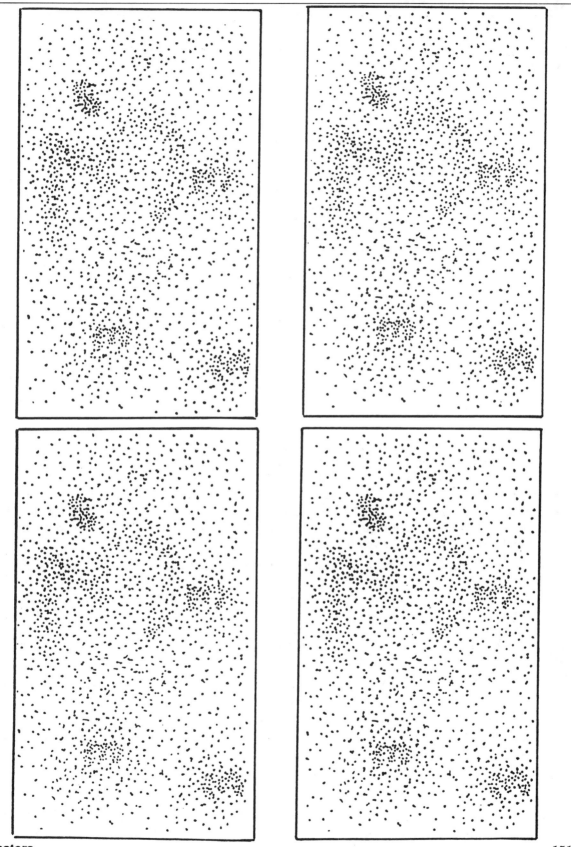

Master 4-4

WHAT DO YOU SEE

Study the picture below for fifteen seconds and then answer the question at the bottom of the picture.

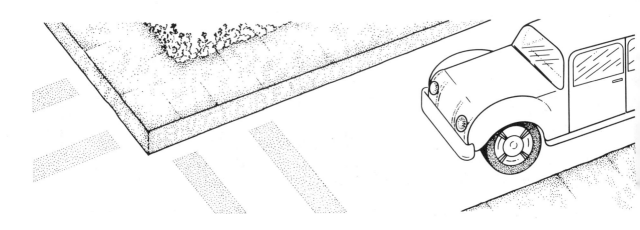

Which of the following words comes to mind when looking at the picture above?
Choose one. a) bee b) ant c) spider d) butterfly e) grasshopper

Look at the picture again. If you study the curb, you'll see the word "butterfly" faintly. This is an example of a subliminal message. Did you choose the word "butterfly"? If so, do you think the subliminal message influenced you to choose "butterfly"?

Testing only yourself is obviously not enough evidence for or against the influence of subliminal messages. Try showing the picture to twenty people -- one at a time. Allow each of them exactly fifteen seconds to study the picture and then have them answer the question. Your subjects may complain that none of the words comes to mind. Insist that they choose one. According to the subliminal persuasion theory, no word SHOULD come to the mind at a conscious level. But, according to the theory, the hidden message will still be recorded by the brain and will still influence the brain's choice of a word.

Record your subjects' answers and then analyze your results. Do your results support the theory of subliminal persuasion, or not? What conclusions, if any, can you draw? Discuss.

Imagine that you did the experiment again and got basically the same type of results--but this time you used several pictures and thousands of subjects instead of just twenty. How would this affect your conclusions?

You may need to fold this sheet in half so your subjects will not be able to read these instructions.

Master 4-5

WHAT DO YOU SEE

Study the picture below for fifteen seconds and then answer the question at the bottom of the picture.

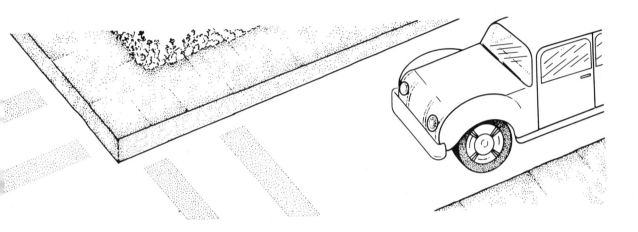

Which of the following words comes to mind when looking at the picture above?
Choose one: a) bee b) ant c) spider d) butterfly e) grasshopper

This time, the word "bee" is embedded in the curb. Show THIS picture to twenty people and compare your results with the results from the "butterfly" picture.

Again, fold this sheet in half so your subjects cannot read the explanation above.

Master 5-1

CHAPTER 5 LEARNING GOALS

1. What is the difference between motivation and emotion?

2. What are the major functions of the following: hypothalamus? reticular formation? pituitary gland? adrenal gland? gonads?

3. What two things are needed for digestion?

4. What are four factors that cause hunger?

5. How do external cues and set points control weight?

6. What are two other possible reasons why someone might be overweight?

7. What cues does the hypothalamus use to determine thirst?

8. How does learning affect thirst?

9. What four psychological needs affect motivation?

10. According to Maslow, how does one advance from one level of needs to another?

11. What are the main differences between the three theories of emotions discussed in the chapter?

MASLOW'S HIERARCHY OF NEEDS

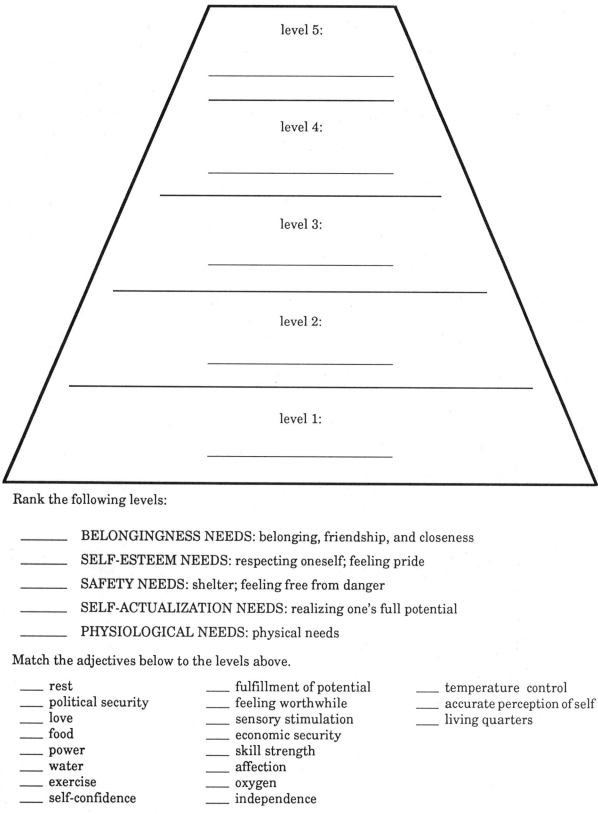

level 5:

_____

_____

level 4:

_____

_____

level 3:

_____

_____

level 2:

_____

_____

level 1:

_____

Rank the following levels:

_____ BELONGINGNESS NEEDS: belonging, friendship, and closeness

_____ SELF-ESTEEM NEEDS: respecting oneself; feeling pride

_____ SAFETY NEEDS: shelter; feeling free from danger

_____ SELF-ACTUALIZATION NEEDS: realizing one's full potential

_____ PHYSIOLOGICAL NEEDS: physical needs

Match the adjectives below to the levels above.

____ rest
____ political security
____ love
____ food
____ power
____ water
____ exercise
____ self-confidence

____ fulfillment of potential
____ feeling worthwhile
____ sensory stimulation
____ economic security
____ skill strength
____ affection
____ oxygen
____ independence

____ temperature control
____ accurate perception of self
____ living quarters

Master 6-1

CHAPTER 6 LEARNING GOALS

1. What is a construct?

2. In what way is consciousness a construct?

3. What is the difference between the subconscious and the unconscious?

4. What does chronobiology study?

5. What are biological clocks? What happens when these clocks ignore the environment? What happens when these clocks are influenced or changed by the environment (schedules, and so on)?

6. What is circadian rhythm?

7. Why is it important to sleep according to a schedule?

8. When does the twilight state of sleep occur?

9. What are several differences between REM and NREM sleep?

10. What are some differences between beta, alpha, and delta waves?

11. What are three hypotheses about why we dream?

12. During what period of sleep do people experience nightmares?

13. Why do some people experience REM rebound?

14. What are incubus attacks and during what sleep period do they occur?

15. During what stage of sleep do people sleepwalk and sleeptalk?

16. What are the symptoms and causes of the following sleep disorders:

    Insomnia? Narcolepsy? Sleep apnea?

17. In general, how does hypnosis affect one's attention? Do people fall asleep during hypnosis?

18. How is meditation similar to hypnosis?

Master 6-2

A DREAM ASSIGNMENT

PART 1   DAY JOURNAL

- Every other day or so in class, I'll ask you to take out your journal and then allow you about ten minutes to fill up a page. If you don't fill up an ENTIRE page in the allotted ten minutes, finish it at home.

- For every two pages written in class, you are responsible for filling up ONE page at home. At home, write about anything you want. Just don't fall behind.

- Don't spend much more than ten minutes on any page. Your pen or pencil should flow freely. Don't worry about grammar, spelling, and so on. Concentrate on content, on getting in touch with your feelings.

- Date all your entries.

PART 2   DREAM JOURNAL

Keep a dream journal for the next two to three weeks.

> Hints: a) before falling asleep, DECIDE you are going to remember your dreams; be patient; it may take 3-4 nights for your unconscious to get the message. BELIEVE.
> b) keep journal and pen close to your bed—write down dreams as soon as possible.

WHAT SHOULD YOU RECORD? Basically, everything: record the dreams you recall immediately, without interpretation; interpretation will come later in part 3.

To be more specific, write down:

- a) dialogue or any words
- b) # of people
- c) types of people—mainly strangers? relatives? friends?
- d) unusual or recurring objects
- e) mood of dream
- f) point of view
- g) settings

If it's difficult to record a dream in writing, sketch a picture.

(cont.)

Master 6-2 (cont.)

PART 3   WRITTEN REPORT

Reread both journals and synthesize them into an organized report. Here are several questions you might want to address in your written report:

- WERE THERE ANY COMMON THREADS, COMMON IDEAS, RUNNING THROUGH EITHER JOURNAL?

- CONTRAST THE IDEAS IN BOTH JOURNALS; ANY SIGNIFICANT DIFFERENCES? WHAT SEEMS TO BE THE MAIN FUNCTION OF YOUR DREAMS?

- ARE YOUR DREAMS BIZARRE? MUNDANE? WHAT DOES THIS TELL YOU ABOUT YOUR PERSONALITY?

- WHICH DREAMS WERE MOST DISTURBING? WHY? WHAT DO THEY MEAN TO YOU?

- WHAT COMMON SYMBOLS OR OBJECTS DID YOU RECORD? WHAT DO YOU THINK THESE SYMBOLS MEAN?

- WERE YOU ABLE TO CONTROL YOUR DREAMS AS YOU REMEMBERED MORE AND MORE OF THEM?

- HOW ARE YOUR DREAMS RELEVANT TO YOUR WAKING LIFE?

- WAS THE CONTENT OF BOTH JOURNALS IDENTICAL ON ANY DAYS? WHAT DOES THIS TELL YOU?

In other words, what did you learn about yourself by writing in your journals?

BRIEFLY summarize the dreams you discuss in your report. Hand in all three parts by _____
If there are any journal or dream entries that you do NOT want read, please mark these "Personal."

Master 7-1

CHAPTER 7 LEARNING GOALS

1. What were Ivan Pavlov's original research intentions? What three strange things helped alter these intentions?

2. In classical conditioning, what causes some kind of reaction or "response"?

3. What automatically and involuntarily produces an unconditional response?

4. After learning has taken place, what automatically and involuntarily produces a conditioned response?

5. What did John Watson "teach" Little Albert? What conclusions did Watson draw from these experiments with Little Albert?

6. What did Mary Jones discover?

7. What is the difference between classical conditioning and operant conditioning?

8. According to B.F. Skinner, why do we perform certain behaviors?

9. How do reinforcements affect behavior?

10. What is the difference between a primary and a secondary reinforcer?

11. What is the difference between positive and negative reinforcement?

12. How does punishment affect behavior?

13. How is generalization different than discrimination learning?

14. In what way is reinforcement used in shaping?

15. What is chaining?

16. How is continuous reinforcement different than partial reinforcement?

17. WHEN is reinforcement given for each of the following schedules of reinforcement: Variable ratio? Fixed ratio? Variable interval? Fixed interval?

18. How does Albert Bandura's theory of social learning differ from classical and operant conditioning?

19. How does the cognitive approach differ from classical and operant conditioning?

20. According to the cognitive approach, what two techniques do people use to learn or solve problems?

Master 7-2

CLASSICAL CONDITIONING

Read each of the following examples and fill in the blanks below each example.

1. Tactless Tom yells at Emotional Ernie. As a result, Ernie's blood pressure automatically rises. The next time that Ernie sees Tom, Ernie's blood pressure rises.

(N) _____ + (UCS) _____ (UCR) _____

(CS) _____ (CR) _____

2. Two practical jokers want to get a horse to involuntarily "go wild" (the horse's heart races, and so on) every time the horse hears "whoa." The jokers will kick the horse in order to train him.

(N) _____ + (UCS) _____ (UCR) _____

(CS) _____ (CR) _____

3. The same practical jokers want to make a dog afraid of a cat by shocking the dog every time he sees the cat.

(N) _____ + (UCS) _____ (UCR) _____

(CS) _____ (CR) _____

4. As a child, Joni's mother would ring a bell every time she gave Joni medicine. The medicine naturally produced an upset stomach. Nowadays, every time Joni hears a bell, her stomach becomes queasy and upset.

(N) _____ + (UCS) _____ (UCR) _____

(CS) _____ (CR) _____

Master 8-1

CHAPTER 8 LEARNING GOALS

1. How does attention affect the brain and learning?

2. What is a learning curve?

3. How do stimulants and depressants affect learning?

4. How can anxiety affect learning?

5. What is state-dependent learning?

6. In general, how do emotional factors affect learning?

7. How does positive transfer differ from negative transfer?

8. What is meant by information processing?

9. How does a schema help one solve problems?

10. How does elaboration improve memory?

11. What is the main reason for using mnemonic devices? How do the following devices help in storing information: Method of Location? Acronym? Narrative Chaining?

12. What does principle learning mean?

13. How does chunking improve memory?

14. What is the definition of forgetting?

15. What is a forgetting curve? How does overlearning affect this curve?

16. What are some differences between recognition and recall?

17. How does interference theory explain forgetting?

18. In general, where or in what is memory physically stored?

19. What are two explanations for amnesia?

20. What are several characteristics of short- and long-term memory?

21. What is the sensory memory system? How do iconic and acoustic memory contribute to the sensory memory system?

22. What is eidetic imagery?

23. Why is eyewitness memory so poor? How does hypnosis affect eyewitness memory?

24. Are people usually successful in identifying faces in a crisis? Why or why not?

Master 8-2

THE ASSAILANT!

Answer question #1 if you saw photographs of the "assailant." Answer #1A if you did NOT see any photographs.

1. Circle the number of the photograph that most resembles the assailant.

   1   2   3   4   5

1A. Write a brief description of the assailant's physical characteristics.

   _____

2. Did you see a clenched fist during the confrontation?

   a) yes   b) no

3. Did you see the scar on the assailant's face?

   a) yes   b) no

4. Approximately how old was the assailant? _____

5. What was the assailant wearing?

   _____

6. What did the assailant say?

   _____

7. Did the assailant ever touch your teacher?

   a) yes   b) no

8. Did you hear when the assailant swore at your teacher?

   a) yes   b) no

Master 8-3

THE ASSAILANT!

Answer question #1 if you saw photographs of the "assailant." Answer #1A if you did NOT see any photographs.

1. Circle the number of the photograph that most resembles the assailant.

    1   2   3   4   5

1A. Write a brief description of the assailant's physical characteristics.

    _____
    .

2. Did you see the clenched fist during the confrontation?

    a) yes   b) no

3. Did you see a scar on the assailant's face?

    a) yes   b) no

4. Approximately how old was the assailant?   _____

5. What was the assailant wearing?

    _____

6. What did the assailant say?

    _____

7. Did you see when the assailant touched your teacher?

    a) yes   b) no

8. Did the assailant ever swear at your teacher?

    a) yes   b) no

Master 8-4

TOUCH VS. TOUCH-AND-TASTE RECALL

DATA SHEET

Check one:

_____ My partner will only touch each item.

_____ My partner will both touch AND taste each item.

Directions ───

Part 1.

Hand the following items in the following order to your partner, tell your partner the new name of the item, and spell the new name twice. Allow your partner exactly 20 seconds to mentally store the new name of the item before presenting the next item.

Part 2.

Hand the following items in the following order to your partner to test your partner's recall. Mark your partner's responses. There is no time limit for this part of the experiment.

ITEMS	NEW NAMES
1. peanut	tren
2. popcorn	snop
3. cracker	berc
4. cereal flake	pelm
5. chocolate	corf
6. pretzel	zunt
7. marshmellow	larn
8. sunflower seed	nerp
9. raisin	tilp

ITEMS	NEW NAMES	PARTNER'S RESPONSES
1. pretzel	zunt	_____
2. chocolate	corf	_____
3. peanut	tren	_____
4. cereal flake	pelm	_____
5. raisin	tilp	_____
6. popcorn	snop	_____
7. marshmellow	larn	_____
8. cracker	berc	_____
9. sunflower seed	nerp	_____

Master 9-1

CHAPTER 9 LEARNING GOALS

1. How did psychologists in the late 1800's try to measure intelligence?

2. How is intelligence usually defined today?

3. What was Alfred Binet's original intention in devising an intelligence test?

4. What did Binet finally decide were four important elements of intelligence?

5. How is an intelligence quotient calculated?

6. What was David Wechsler's original intention in devising an intelligence test?

7. How was Wechsler's test different than Binet's?

8. What three parts make up the Wechsler Adult Intelligence Scale (WAIS)?

9. Who or what influences the definition of intelligence? In what way?

10. Is intelligence inherited?

11. What are the differences between individual intelligence tests and group intelligence tests?

12. What restrictions do courts place on the use of I.Q. tests?

13. Does brain size influence intelligence in ANY way?

14. How does mental challenge affect the brain?

15. What is set and how does it affect creativity?

16. What does it mean to break set?

17. What would an I.Q. of 79 mean? 19 or below?

18. What are several common and uncommon causes of mental retardation?

19. Which factors in the environment seem to lead to retardation?

20. What are several methods of treatment for the mentally retarded?

Master 9-2

CREATIVITY

Directions. Write down as many uses as possible for each of the four objects listed below. You will be allowed exactly 5 minutes to complete this exercise. You MUST stop writing as soon as you hear the announcement that 5 minutes have elapsed.

chalkboard eraser	crayon	coffee can	bicycle tire

This is a fun exercise that you can complete in 5 minutes. Look at the four objects listed below and think of as many uses as possible for each object. Just do your best.

chalkboard eraser	crayon	coffee can	bicycle tire

Master 10-1

CHAPTER 10 LEARNING GOALS

1. What is the difference between nature and nurture?

2. Why do identical twins have identical heredity? What conclusions have scientists drawn from years of studies of identical twins?

3. What conclusions about development did scientists draw from the chimpanzee studies described in the chapter?

4. What is the definition of maturation?

5. In general, can the maturation process be sped up considerably in any way? If so, how? If not, why not? Can the maturation process be slowed? If so, how? If not, why not?

6. What are growth cycles?

7. What is "imprinted" onto an animal's brain at a certain point in its development?

8. What is the relationship between imprinting and critical periods?

9. What is the difference between a nuclear family and an extended family?

10. If mothers work outside the home, does this seem to have a negative effect on the children? Why or why not?

11. Does the absence of the father in the home generally have a negative effect on the children?

12. What are several reasons why parents abuse their children?

13. What is separation anxiety? Is it normal? Is it universal?

14. What cognitive abilities does a child have at each of Piaget's four stages of cognitive development?

15. How do people decide right and wrong if they are in Kohlberg's preconventional level? Conventional level? Postconventional level?

16. Why did "Genie's" speech level not improve beyond that of a child aged four or five?

Master 11-1

CHAPTER 11 LEARNING GOALS

1. At what ages does adolescence usually begin and end?

2. What is the age range for early, middle, and late adolescence?

3. How do hormones affect the body?

4. Which three glands are particularly active during puberty?

5. Do adolescents handle puberty and growth spurts easily?

6. How do boys and girls react to being early maturers? Late maturers?

7. What is a rite of passage? What are subcultures and why are they formed in our society?

8. What are the differences between crowds, cliques, and gangs?

9. According to Erik Erikson, what is the main conflict of adolescence?

10. How does Erikson define fidelity?

11. According to James Marcia, what are 4 possible identity states in which adolescents can fit? What are several differences between the 4 states?

12. What new abilities do people acquire when they reach Jean Piaget's formal operations stage of cognitive development?

13. How do people in Lawrence Kohlberg's post-conventional level decide right and wrong?

14. How does the adolescent's time perspective change as he or she matures from early to middle to late adolescence?

15. On what issues do parents and adolescents tend to agree? On what issues is there less agreement?

16. How do arguments between parents and adolescents change as adolescents mature from early to middle to late adolescence?

17. What is the connection between sexual maturity and independence?

Master 12-1

CHAPTER 12 LEARNING GOALS

1. Approximately how long does early adulthood last?

2. How does society view "man's work"? On what do women focus during their mid 20's?

3. In what ways do men and women need to "prove" themselves during their 20's?

4. Why do people become so depressed and frustrated during their 20's?

5. Why do stress and a sense of urgency occur between 30 to 35 years?

6. Is a midlife crisis inevitable?

7. How does the midlife transition affect marriage?

8. How do male and female priorities shift during middle adulthood?

9. Do most women experience an empty-nest period? What are the characteristics of those women who DO experience this problem?

10. What is menopause? How does it affect women?

11. What is the study of old people called?

12. How do internal time clocks affect aging?

13. What usually causes memory problems for old people?

14. Does intelligence automatically decline with age? Why do older people do relatively poorly on I.Q. tests?

15. What is senility? Is it inevitable with old age? What is the major cause of senility?

16. What is cerebral arteriosclerosis?

17. What are three major fears of old people?

18. Are most old people less active after retirement? Why or why not?

19. Are the majority of old people isolated and lonely?

20. Why do many old people view themselves as a burden?

21. Do most old people live in an institution?

22. What is the study of death called?

23. What are three major fears of the terminally ill?

24. According to Elisabeth Kubler-Ross, what stages do terminally ill people go through?

25. What is the main criticism of Ross's theory?

26. What is a hospice?

Master 13-1

CHAPTER 13 LEARNING GOALS

1. To what does the word gender refer?

2. Which gender has more androgen? More estrogen?

3. In general, how do androgen and estrogen affect behavior?

4. In what way could a male become "pregnant"?

5. Can females be just as aggressive as males?

6. Which gender tends to be more naturally active?

7. What are spatial skills? Which gender PERFORMS better at spatial skills? Is this better performance related to differences in the brain?

8. What four factors need to be resolved before concluding that one gender is better at math than another?

9. What is one environmental factor that might help determine why males do better at math than females?

10. Do males and females differ in their self-confidence?

11. According to studies, are there any significant differences between males' and females' desire to achieve?

12. Do women seem to possess a maternal instinct?

13. What happens to a woman's body during menstruation?

14. What are several possible symptoms of premenstrual syndrome?

15. How does marriage affect many women's happiness level? Men's happiness level?

16. Who are more miserable, divorced women or divorced men?

17. What is gender role identification? What kind of gender role identification tends to lead to the most "normal" people?

18. What characteristics would an androgynous person have?

24. How do Albert Bandura's ideas differ from Skinner's?

25. In general, how does humanism differ from psychoanalysis and behaviorism?

26. According to Carl Rogers, what is the biggest problem people face?

27. According to Abraham Maslow, what does it mean to be self-actualized?

28. What is one major criticism of humanism?

29. What is a personality trait?

30. What three traits appear at any early age and remain constant over time?

Master 15-1

CHAPTER 15 LEARNING GOALS

1. What is a psychological test? Why do psychologists use them?

2. In what two ways are norms established? What do norms show psychologists?

3. When is a test valid?

4. What is test reliability?

5. What is a personality inventory? Which personality inventory is used most often in school?

6. How can you fool a personality inventory?

7. What is theoretically "projected" when someone takes a projective test?

8. Why is the Rorschach test not reliable or valid?

9. What are two possible uses of projective tests?

10. In general, what do aptitude tests measure?

11. What three categories are commonly included in aptitude tests?

12. What do achievement tests measure? What do they NOT predict?

13. What is the main reason that the SAT test is controversial? What are some positive things about the test?

14. What is the most common vocational interest test used? In general, how does it work?

15. How do the halo effect, the reverse halo effect, and standoutishness affect interviews?

16. What is situational assessment? What is one drawback of using situational assessment?

17. What are three ethical standards of testing?

18. What is meant by the term "Barnum effect"?

RESUME

DENISE SMITH
16 YEARS OLD
GRADE POINT AVERAGE: 2.1 (C-)
JOB OBJECTIVE: COMPUTER PROGRAMMER
JOB EXPERIENCE:

On the weekends, Denise is a frequent volunteer at a nursing home in the area. She enjoys working with the residents and feels that she is contributing something important. Denise had a regular job for a few months as a waitress, but she quit because she didn't have enough time to study.

Using the scale below, how would you rate Denise's:

_____ a. Friendliness

_____ b. Honesty

_____ c. Generosity

_____ d. Confidence level

_____ e. Chances of succeeding as a computer programmer

1	2	3	4	5
poor	below average	average	above average	excellent

Master 15-3

RESUME

DENISE SMITH
16 YEARS OLD
GRADE POINT AVERAGE: 4.1 (A-)
JOB OBJECTIVE: COMPUTER PROGRAMMER
JOB EXPERIENCE:

On the weekends, Denise is a frequent volunteer at a nursing home in the area. She enjoys working with the residents and feels that she is contributing something important. Denise had a regular job for a few months as a waitress, but she quit because she didn't have enough time to study.

Using the scale below, how would you rate Denise's:

_____ a. Friendliness

_____ b. Honesty

_____ c. Generosity

_____ d. Confidence level

_____ e. Chances of succeeding as a computer programmer

1	2	3	4	5
poor	below average	average	above average	excellent

Master 16-1

CHAPTER 16 LEARNING GOALS

1. What is frustration?

2. When do we experience conflict? What are four types of conflict and what choice needs to be made for each?

3. What is anxiety? When does anxiety occur?

4. What is stress? When does it arise?

5. What is the difference between eustress and distress? What determines whether a stress is eustress or distress?

6. What kind of reaction to stress do lower animals experience?

7. What kind of response to stress do humans experience?

8. How does the Social Readjustment Rating Scale help to predict disease and sickness?

9. Other than life changes, what two other factors may lead to stress?

10. Is it okay to bottle up your feelings?

11. What are several differences between a Type A and a Type B personality?

12. What is meant by a general adaptation syndrome? What three stages make up THE general adaptation syndrome?

13. What four major factors may lead to substance abuse?

14. How do drugs affect the firing of nerve cells?

15. What is the chemical effect of alcohol?

16. What are four physical effects of alcohol?

17. When do people experience a synergistic effect?

18. What are six indicators of alcoholism?

19. What are two keys to ending alcoholism?

20. What are two drawbacks of labeling alcoholism a disease?

21. Why is marijuana called a psychedelic? What are several effects, real and suggested, of using marijuana? Which of these effects is most serious?

22. Why is tolerance dangerous? What is paranoia and what may cause it?

23. What are several effects of using cocaine? What does it mean to have a psychchological dependence on cocaine?

24. What are opiates? How do they affect the brain? How do they make a person feel? What does it mean to have a physical dependence on opiates?

25. Why is LSD called a hallucinogen?

26. What are steroids? How do steroids affect the body? What are some problems with using steroids?

27. How do most males and most females commit suicide? Which gender is most successful in committing suicide?

28. What stressors may lead to suicide?

29. What is the leading cause of teenage death?

Master 19-1

CHAPTER 19 LEARNING GOALS

1. When did hospitals for the insane begin to become more humane? Who contributed to this change and how?

2. What are the main differences between counseling and clinical psychologists? What are some differences in their educational backgrounds?

3. What is the main difference between a psychiatrist and a psychologist?

4. What do psychiatric social workers do for patients? How do psychiatric nurses differ from registered nurses?

5. What is psychotherapy? What are four goals of therapists during psychotherapy?

6. How much treatment time is involved in psychoanalysis?

7. According to psychoanalysts, what causes anxiety and guilt?

8. How does free association work? What is the goal of free association?

9. What is transference? Why do some patients use transference during psychoanalytic treatment?

10. According to humanistic therapy, what is the function of the therapist? Why is this therapy called "humanistic"?

11. Why do humanists use the word CLIENT rather than PATIENT?

12. Why is Rogerian therapy also called nondirective therapy? In what way does a nondirective therapist act like a mirror?

13. What is unconditional positive regard? Why is it critical during humanistic therapy?

14. How do behaviorists view most mental disorders?

15. How long does behavioral therapy usually last? For what kinds of problems is behavioral therapy not very effective?

16. How does systematic desensitization work? What is the goal of this desensitization?

17. What is the goal of aversive conditioning? How does it work?

18. What is a token economy? How do people in a token economy system receive tokens?

19. How did cognitive behavioral therapy get its name?

20. According to Albert Ellis, what two components make up humans? Why is his therapy called rational emotive therapy?

21. What do people need to do if they are guilty of awfulizing their internal sentences?

22. What are two purposes of group therapy?

23. What is the main purpose of encounter groups?

24. What are three factors that all therapies have in common?

25. What are four ways that patients benefit from therapy?

26. What is chemotherapy?

27. What is electroconvulsive therapy? What physical changes occur as a result of this therapy? For what disorder does ECT work best?

28. What is psychosurgery? What are two dangers of psychosurgery?

Master 20-1

CHAPTER 20 LEARNING GOALS

1. What human process does attribution theory explain?

2. What are three parts of the attribution theory and what happens during each part?

3. What physical symptoms occur during "falling in love"? How do these physical symptoms lead to emotional and mental associations?

4. What two main factors affect liking and loving? In what ways?

5. What guidelines should one follow in revealing oneself to another person?

6. In what way might aggression and violence today be natural? Why might aggression and violence be the result of imitation?

7. In what way might aggression be a product of some symbolic issue?

8. What is deindividuation? How might it lead to aggression?

9. Why do some people feel more powerful when in a group? What is this phenomenon called?

10. What part of the brain may influence aggression?

11. How can allergies and amphetamines lead to aggression?

12. What two principles have emerged from basic film studies?

13. What does imitation learning tell us about violence and TV? What is the clear short-term effect of violent TV?

14. About how many actual laboratory studies have been done on the effects of TV on violence?

15. How is behavior observed in field studies? What have field studies told us about TV and violence?

16. How is data gathered for correlational studies? What have correlational studies told us about TV and violence?

17. What are two main conclusions about TV and violence?

18. What is catharsis? How CAN catharsis reduce aggression? DOES catharsis seem to reduce aggression?

19. After interviewing subjects in helping experiments, what two things were found?

20. In what way does "number of people" affect helping behavior during emergencies?

21. What are five general conclusions about why people help or do not help in emergencies?

22. What is evaluation apprehension? How does it affect helping behavior?

23. What is the difference between crowding and density?

Master 20-2

CHANGING CAREERS

Read the description below and answer the two questions beneath it.

Melissa Weeber is 28-years old. She has been a high school counselor for six years. She enjoys the job, but feels that her role has been reduced to simply scheduling students for classes. She now wants to become a marriage counselor. When asked to describe her, her students commonly use the following adjectives: caring, dependable, and hard-working.

How would you rate this person's chances of becoming an effective marriage counselor?

1	2	3	4	5	6	7	8	9
extremely low	very low	low	below average	average	above average	high	very high	excellent

If you were responsible for hiring this person as a marriage counselor, what would be the likelihood of you hiring her?

1	2	3	4	5
very low	low	average	high	very high

Master 20-3

CHANGING CAREERS

Read the description below and answer the two questions beneath it.

Melissa Weeber is 28-years old. She has been a high school counselor for six years. She enjoys the job, but feels that her role has been reduced to simply scheduling students for classes. She now wants to become a marriage counselor. When asked to describe her, her students commonly use the following adjectives: efficient, dependable, and hard-working.

How would you rate this person's chances of becoming an effective marriage counselor?

1	2	3	4	5	6	7	8	9
extremely low	very low	low	below average	average	above average	high	very high	excellent

If you were responsible for hiring this person as a marriage counselor, what would be the likelihood of you hiring her?

1	2	3	4	5
very low	low	average	high	very high

Master 21-1

CHAPTER 21 LEARNING GOALS

1. What does it mean to internalize attitudes and beliefs? What determines how strongly one internalizes attitudes and beliefs?

2. What is a reference group? What do reference groups provide for us?

3. What is a stereotype? What are two purposes of stereotypes?

4. Can stereotypes be avoided? When do stereotypes become dangerous? What is prejudice?

5. What happens when we form illusory correlations?

6. What are two "positive sides" of prejudice? What kind of prejudice seems to be decreasing?

7. What happens during the process of scapegoating?

8. What is congnitive dissonance? What is one way of overcoming it?

9. What is one theory about why people obeyed authority in Stanley Milgram's experiment?

10. What is immunization? What is one way to immunize someone against propaganda? What is one way to decrease immunization against propaganda?

11. In regards to persuasion, which is more important, what a person says or how it is said?

12. What does the polygraph measure? Does it determine whether a person is lying?

13. What are two reasons why the accuracy of the polygraph is controversial?

14. How does friendliness by captors affect prisoners?

15. How is sensory deprivation sometimes accomplished?

16. How does the brain react to sensory deprivation?

17. Why does a reward system for prisoners often become destructive?

18. What is one technique that advertisers use to "brainwash" consumers?

MEMORY TEST

How many times were each of the following word pairs read?

1. cat-meow   _____

2. table-coat   _____

3. milk-tea   _____

4. fork-spoon   _____

5. dirt-wood   _____

6. wallet-ankle   _____

7. cricket-stocking _____

8. brick-house   _____

9. gamble-bed   _____

10. football-field   _____

11. bacon-eggs   _____

12. tree-carpet   _____

13. wing-bird   _____

14. money-toilet   _____

Master 21-3

ILLUSORY CORRELATIONS DATA SHEET

Transfer the answers to the "Memory Test" you just completed to the list below.

FAMILIAR WORD PAIRS

#1 (cat-meow) : _____

#4 (fork-spoon): _____

#8 (brick-house): _____

#11 (bacon-eggs): _____

#13 (wing-bird): _____

TOTAL A: _____

UNFAMILIAR WORD PAIRS

#2 (table-coat): _____

#6 (wallet-ankle): _____

#9 (gamble-bed): _____

#12 (tree-carpet): _____

#14 (money-toilet): _____

TOTAL B: _____

Section
4

*Coordinating A Psychology Fair
At Your School*

COORDINATING A PSYCHOLOGY FAIR AT YOUR SCHOOL

If you've ever attended a Psychology Fair, this is what probably happened. You and several students travelled to a local high school and registered. Throughout the day you heard expert speakers lecturing about various issues in psychology. Some of the speakers were good; some were not so good. Overall, the Fair was worthwhile and interesting to both you and your students. If this is the kind of fair you'd like to coordinate, get a firm commitment from your speakers as early as possible. If you're going to pay your speakers by charging money to participating schools, collect the money early and find out how many students from each school will attend. And be organized.

The format described above is certainly a worthwhile one, but it has its limitations, the most obvious being that participants don't really participate much; they listen. The rest of this section will describe a format in which participants DO participate. Imagine a gymnasium filled with fifty student projects, or booths, where participants stroll around solving puzzles, answering questions, observing trained mice. In the middle of the gym is a giant cardboard maze through which participants weave and wind, searching for an exit. In other words, participants acquire "hand-on" experience. In this case, the participants will be students from your school who attend the Fair during their free periods.

WHY HAVE A PSYCHOLOGY FAIR?

One, it's genuinely fun—not only for you, but for your students and participants as well. Two, your students will become authorities on their topics—a truer sign of learning than any test score. Three, it will communicate to your students and to the rest of the school something YOU already know—that psychology is exciting. Four, it will put into practice some of the ideas that you discuss in class. For instance, you and your students will set GOALS for the fair and VISUALIZE these goals; there will be times when you'll need to MOTIVATE your students. Finally, it's good public relations, which may affect enrollment in Psychology. This is not to suggest that increasing enrollment should be a goal, but it's a nice benefit.

HOW TO GET STARTED

1) Mention the fair to your students. If they're not excited, well...

2) Okay, they're excited! Now mention the fair to the administration. They need to promise two things: a)that you can use the gym, or whatever room, for the entire day of the fair and the night before to prepare; and b)that you can have students excused from school for the entire day so they can work at their booths. If the administration agrees...

3) Sell the fair to your students. Brainstorm for booth ideas. What would they like to see at THEIR fair? It's always a pleasure to see how innovative and creative students can be. Remember, during brainstorming sessions, ALL ideas are good ideas. Accumulate more booth ideas than you need, however, since some will not be practical.

4) Allow students a few days to think of even more ideas. They can skim through the text or they can pore through back issues of PSYCHOLOGY TODAY or other appropriate magazines. Perhaps you can allow them a day or two in class to skim through several sources that you may have. Then have a second brainstorming session. (These brainstorming sessions will probably be more productive near the end of the course rather than at the beginning.)

5) Pare down your list. Throw out impractical ideas. Refine the ones that may work.

6) Begin to obtain commitments from students regarding which projects they'd like to do. If you don't have many students, each student can be responsible for one booth; if you do, perhaps they can work in pairs. To solidify their commitments, you might want to draw up a simple contract that outlines their responsibilities.

7) If you decide that you want to include a giant, cardboard maze, begin contacting refrigerator outlet stores for boxes. You'll need about 80 boxes for a 50-foot by 40-foot maze; needless to say, it will take several months to collect all these boxes. Designing a maze is relatively simple. Take a piece of graph paper and sketch several possibilities. You want to make it difficult enough to challenge people, but you don't want to make it so difficult that it becomes impossible to construct.

The actual construction should take about four or five hours—which means that you need to construct it the night before. Transfer the maze you've drawn on your graph paper onto the gym floor using masking tape. This will only take about ten minutes. Cut open one corner of the first box, open it up, and place it upright, forming a 90 degree angle, or an "L." Place it at one of the corners of the maze and tape the bottom flaps of the box to the floor. (Most refrigerator boxes have a six-inch flap at the top and bottom of them.) Attach a second box to the first one, a third box to the second one, and so on, forming as many right angles as possible. To actually attach the boxes together, you can punch holes where the two boxes slightly overlap and use thick plastic wire to tie them together—similar to how you would use a "twist-tie" at the top of a garbage bag. (This think plastic wire is often used by electricians who call it "tie-wire." A hardware store would have it.) To anchor different sections of the maze, you can place tables just outside of it and tie the maze to the tables. You will need about ten students to help you. If all this sounds like a gargantuan task, find one or two other teachers who will volunteer to supervise or work.

Possible hypothesis: Subjects' expectations will influence their performance in the maze. Tell one third of the subjects that the maze is extremely difficult; tell another third that the maze is simple; simply tell the final third to go through. Then time all subjects to see which group performs best. (Once you've collected enough data—which will not take long since there will be long lines of people waiting to get in—stop instructing subjects about the difficulty of the maze and simply list everyone's time on a big poster just outside the maze. You can conduct an informal contest to see who can make it through the maze most quickly!)

A final note: You will need to organize the line leading up to the maze, similar to what is done for rides at an amusement park.

BOOTH IDEAS

The primary question you have probably involves the kind of projects that students can do. Tell students that each project should encourage participation and each project should teach something through that participation. Below is a very general list of project ideas.

Students can:

1) Contact a graphologist who will show them how to analyze handwriting. These students can then provide brief analyses of participants' handwriting (with disclaimers about accuracy, of course).

2) Illustrate several perceptual illusions and explain why they fool us. For example, someone can build an Ames Room. There are so many kinds of illusions that several students can do a project on this topic.

3) Explain how interference can affect learning.

4) Train a mouse in a Skinner box. Make sure all mice are accounted for afterwards!

5) Show how proxemics studies nonverbal behavior. Participants can look at two pictures on either side of this booth. In one picture, the person's eyes will be open; in the other they will be closed. In front of which picture will participants stand closer? Participants can be given a task (count the buttons on the shirt) to ensure that they walk to both pictures.

6) Conduct a mirror tracing exercise.

7) Illustrate how subliminal messages are used in advertisements and elsewhere.

8) Test participants' potential ESP.

9) Illustrate different types of dream symbolism.

10) Administer various, innocuous intelligence, personality, and interest inventories.

11) Outline the functions of different parts of the brain. Perhaps participants can be tested on reaction time.

12) Test people's problem solving skills with "brain teasers."

13) Test people's sensory skills with taste tests, smell tests, and so on.

14) Illustrate the Zeigarnik effect.

15) Test people's memories. Several students can conduct various memory tests.

16) Teach people relaxation techniques. Perhaps participants can learn how to use biofeedback.

17) Show how advertisers use persuasion, how some cults use brainwashing.

18) Illustrate different forms of body language.

19) Survey participants on various topics and later report the results in the school newspaper.

20) Illustrate how birth order may be related to personality.

21) Build a stereoscope.

FINAL TOUCHES

Consider calling local retailers to see if they will donate prizes for the best projects. Or if you have a booster club at your school, perhaps they will donate them. You should have no problems finding several teachers who would be willing to judge the projects.

Contact a local tee-shirt shop to see if they will give you a discount if you order shirts in bulk. If so, see how many students would be interested in ordering a Psychology Fair tee-shirt! If students think it's a good idea, have a student artist sketch a design for the front. On the backs, students can use psychological nicknames: id, REM, actualized, and so on.

About a week before the Fair, put up signs around the school to publicize it. If you have a cooperative art department, perhaps someone there could design a slick poster for you. The Fair will probably be extremely popular, so you may even want to send a press release to several local newspapers. If your principal permits it, invite people from the community to attend.

Keep in mind that coordinating the Fair will require a great deal of direction and effort on your part. Despite the work involved, however, the results should prove worthwhile and highly rewarding.

Section
5

Answers To Textbook
Review Questions

CHAPTER 1

1. philosophy
2. applied psychologists
3. research psychologists
4. psychology
5. Wilhelm Wundt
6. False
7. False
8. True
9. False
10. True
11. a
12. d
13. e
14. b
15. a
16. e
17. c
18. d
19. b
20. c

CHAPTER 2

1. people are less likely to help if there's a full moon
2. 20 males and 20 females
3. stopping, getting out of car, assisting
4. full moon
5. Group B
6. Group A
7. False
8. True
9. False
10. True
11. d
12. a
13. b
14. f
15. e
16. g
17. f
18. d
19. c
20. a
21. b
22. g
23. c
24. e

CHAPTER 3

1. hemispheres
2. corpus callosum
3. frontal association strip
4. motor strip
5. sensory strip
6. c
7. d
8. a
9. b
10. d
11. a
12. b
13. e
14. c
15. T
16. A
17. T
18. P
19. A
20. P

CHAPTER 4

1. b
2. e
3. c
4. a
5. d
6. R
7. C
8. R
9. C
10. b
11. a
12. c
13. c
14. a
15. c
16. d
17. b
18. a
19. e
20. color constancy
21. space constancy
22. size constacny
23. binocular disparity
24. brightness constancy

CHAPTER 5

1. A
2. R
3. P
4. P
5. A
6. R
7. estrogen
8. gonads
9. estrogen
10. androgens
11. YES
12. YES
13. YES
14. NO
15. YES
16. False
17. True
18. True
19. True
20. c
21. e
22. d
23. b
24. a   26. b
25. c   27. a

CHAPTER 6

1. unconscious
2. chronobiology
3. construct
4. 25
5. entrainment
6. 24
7. consciousness
8. a
9. b
10. a
11. d
12. NREM
13. REM
14. REM
15. NREM
16. REM
17. REM
18. d
19. c
20. a
21. b
22. False
23. False
24. True
25. False   26. True

Answers To Textbook Review Questions

CHAPTER 7

1. OP—operant conditioning
2. SL—social learning
3. CC—classical conditioning
4. SL—social learning
5. CC—classical conditioning
6. OP—operant conditioning
7. needle
8. fear
9. dentist
10. fear
11. dentist
12. secondary reinforcer
13. primary reinforcer
14. primary reinforcer
15. secondary reinforcer
16. positive reinforcement
17. negative reinforcement
18. negative reinforcement
19. positive reinforcement
20. b
21. c
22. a
23. b
24. d
25. a
26. c

CHAPTER 8

1. positive
2. negative
3. state dependent learning
4. schema
5. information processing
6. elaboration
7. principle learning
8. True
9. False
10. False
11. True
12. True
13. RECALL
14. RECOGNITION
15. RECALL
16. BOTH
17. d
18. b
19. a
20. e
21. c
22. b

CHAPTER 9

1. b
2. a
3. a
4. c
5. b
6. c
7. b
8. c
9. a
10. c
11. d
12. True
13. False
14. True
15. False
16. False
17. True
18. True
19. b
20. c
21. d
22. d

CHAPTER 10

1. b
2. a
3. b
4. c
5. d
6. True
7. False
8. False
9. False
10. True
11. True
12. False
13. b
14. c
15. a
16. d
17. a
18. b
19. c
20. b
21. d
22. b
23. b
24. c
25. a
26. c
27. a

CHAPTER 11

1. L
2. E
3. E
4. M
5. M
6. L
7. False
8. True
9. False
10. True
11. True
12. rite of passage
13. alienation
14. identity confusion
15. fidelity
16. moratorium
17. c
18. a
19. d
20. c
21. b
22. d
23. b
24. a

CHAPTER 12

1. True
2. True
3. False
4. True
5. False
6. True
7. True
8. False
9. False
10. thanatology
11. gerontology
12. three
13. arteriosclerosis
14. senile
15. d
16. a
17. b
18. b

CHAPTER 13	CHAPTER 14	CHAPTER 15
1. d	1. c	1. b
2. a	2. d	2. a
3. d	3. b	3. c
4. a	4. c	4. d
5. a	5. b	5. b
6. True	6. c	6. a
7. False	7. a	7. c
8. False	8. b	8. c
9. True	9. a	9. d
10. False	10. d	10. b
11. False	11. a	11. a
12. False	12. d	12. d
13. True	13. superego	13. reliable
14. True	14. free association	14. halo effect
15. True	15. persona	15. norm
16. b	16. neoFreudians	16. validity
17. d	17. Horney	17. situational assessement
18. b	18. intimacy	18. False
	19. self-actualization	19. False
	20. True	20. True
	21. False	21. True
	22. True	22. False
	23. True	

CHAPTER 16

1. c
2. b
3. a
4. d
5. b
6. a
7. d
8. c
9. b
10. d
11. a
12. c
13. True
14. True
15. False
16. True
17. False
18. True
19. False
20. True

CHAPTER 17

1. immune
2. antibodies
3. sudden death phenomenon
4. muscle contraction headaches
5. migraine headaches
6. True
7. True
8. True
9. False
10. True
11. d
12. a
13. c
14. b
15. d
16. d
17. a
18. c
19. b

CHAPTER 18

1. e
2. d
3. a
4. b
5. c
6. False
7. False
8. True
9. False
10. True
11. delusions
12. word salad
13. clang associations
14. mania
15. bipolar
16. a
17. b
18. b
19. c
20. d

CHAPTER 19

1. c
2. b
3. a
4. c
5. d
6. b
7. d
8. c
9. d
10. a
11. b
12. a
13. False
14. False
15. True
16. False
17. False
18. True
19. True

CHAPTER 20

1. d
2. a
3. b
4. e
5. True
6. True
7. True
8. False
9. True
10. False
11. False
12. c
13. d
14. a
15. crowding
16. density
17. evaluation apprehension
18. personal space
19. territoriality

CHAPTER 21

1. stereotype
2. prejudice
3. internalize
4. reference groups
5. scapegoats
6. illusory correlations
7. immunization
8. cognitive dissonance
9. True
10. False
11. True
12. True
13. False
14. True
15. False
16. True

Section 6

Answers To Student Workbook

Chapter 1

ANSWER KEY

Vocabulary Review/Test Preparation

1.	a	6.	c	11.	d	16.	b
2.	c	7.	a	12.	b	17.	d
3.	b	8.	c	13.	c	18.	c
4.	b	9.	a	14.	b	19.	b
5.	d	10.	d	15.	a	20.	d

Vocabulary - See chapter content

Worksheet - Crossword Puzzle.

Chapter 2

ANSWER KEY

Vocabulary

1.	N	6.	B	11.	Q	16.	C
2.	I	7.	D	12.	J	17.	0
3.	F	8.	H	13.	G	18.	L
4.	R	9.	M	14.	E		
5.	K	10.	P	15.	A		

Review/Test Preparation

A. True/False
1. true
2. true
3. false
4. true
5. true

B. Multiple choice
1. d
2. b
3. a
4. c
5. c

C. Fill in the Blanks
1. survey
2. naturalistic observation
3. interview
4. case study
5. cross sectional, longitudinal
6. longitudinal
7. cross sectional
8. Ethical Principles
9. spatial ability
10. field experiments

Worksheet

1. saint, mural, antic: naturalistic
2. stung, heavenly, dorm; survey method
3. invent, weary, thirst; interview
4. sedate, custom, tidy; case study
5. attitude, denial, belong; longitudinal
6. action, seasonal, crest; cross sectional

Chapter 3

ANSWER KEY

Vocabulary

1. dominance
2. axon
3. hypothalamus
4. hormones
5. thyroid gland
6. gonads
7. cerebral cortex
8. hemisphere
9. synapse
10. metabolism
11. reflex
12. androgen
13. sensory strip
14. corpus callosum
15. neurotransmitter
16. cerebellum
17. glands
18. adrenal glands
19. estrogen
20. endocrine system
21. reticular activating system
22. spinal cord
23. visual area
24. lower brain
25. adrenaline
26. pituitary gland
27. neuron
28. thalamus
29. frontal association areas
30. growth hormone
31. dendrite
32. motor strip

Review/Test Preparation

1. b
2. c
3. a
4. b
5. c
6. c
7. d
8. c
9. a
10. b
11. b
12. c
13. d
14. d
15. b
16. a
17. c
18. a
19. a
20. c

Chapter 4

ANSWER KEY

Vocabulary

1.	f	11.	k	21.	cc	31.	jj
2.	q	12.	n	22.	d	32.	z
3.	aa	13.	y	23.	bb	33.	j
4.	ff	14.	gg	24.	o	34.	ee
5.	11	15.	r	25.	1	35.	g
6.	i	16.	c	26.	w	36.	s
7.	a	17.	kk	27.	dd	37.	p
8.	m	18.	b	28.	ii	38.	u
9.	x	19.	v	29.	h	39.	mm
10.	t	20.	hh	30.	e		

Review/Test Preparation

1. sensation, perception
2. white light, light wavelengths
3. cornea, iris, lens, pupil, retina, blind spot, rods, cones, rods, cones, red, bl▸ green
4. color blind, yellow-blue, red-green, color blind
5. afterimage
6. audition, pitch, intensity, decibels
7. eardrum, cochlea, hair cells, auditory nerve
8. cutaneous
9. olfaction, cilia, olfactory bulbs
10. pheromones
11. taste buds, sweet, sour, bitter, salt
12. perception, size, color, brightness, space
13. depth perception, binocular disparity
14. visual texture, similarity, closure
15. illusion
16. subliminal perception, extrasensory perception

Chapter 5

ANSWER KEY

Vocabulary

1. motivation
2. gonads
3. glucose
4. anorexia nervosa
5. James Lange Theory
6. physiological needs
7. reticular formation
8. intrinsic motivation
9. contact comfort
10. hierarchy of needs
11. bulimia
12. manipulation motive
17. testes
18. self esteem
19. adrenal glands
20. emotion
21. cognition
22. safety needs
23. blood sugar level
24. pituitary gland
25. Cannon Bard Theory
26. selfactualization
27. belongingness
28. extrinsic motivation
29. estrogen
30. set point
31. ovaries

Review/Test Preparation

1. true
2. true
3. false
4. true
5. false
6. false
7. true
8. true
9. true
10. false
11. true
12. false
13. true
14. true
15. false
16. true
17. true
18. false
19. false
20. false
21. true
22, true
23. true
24. false
25. false

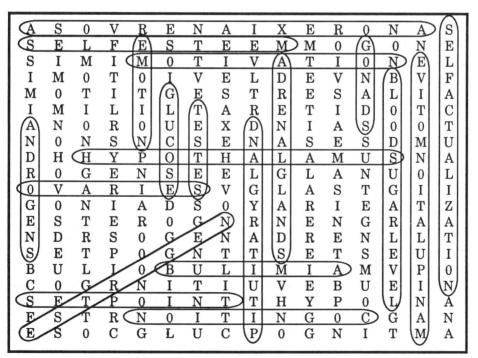

Chapter 5

ANSWER KEY

Worksheet

1. estrogen
2. set point
3. emotion
4. hypothalamus
5. self esteem
6. cognition
7. glucose
8. blood sugar level
9. manipulation motive
10. bulimia

11. gonads
12. ovaries
13. motivation
14. adrenal glands
15. testes
16. andorgens
17. self-actualization
18. anorexia nervosa
19. pituitary gland

Chapter 6

ANSWER KEY

Vocabulary

1.	chronobiology	11.	sleep apnea	21.	entrainment
2.	circadian rhythm	12.	meditation	22.	insomnia
3.	delta waves	13.	construct	23	NREM sleep
4.	narcolepsy	14.	nightmare	24.	social entrainment
5.	consciousness	15.	free-running	25.	beta waves
6.	twilight state	16.	subconscious		
7.	REM rebound	17.	hypnosis		
8.	incubus attack	18.	alpha waves		
9.	biological clocks	19.	trance		
10.	REM sleep	20.	unconscious		

Review/Test Preparation

1.	b	11.	b	21.	c
2.	c	12.	b	22.	d
3.	a	13.	c	23.	true
4.	b	14.	d	24.	false
5.	d	15.	b	25.	true
6.	d	16.	b		
7.	a	17.	c		
8.	b	18.	a		
9.	c	19.	a		
10.	a	20.	b		

Chapter 7

ANSWER KEY

Vocabulary Review

1. classical conditioning
2. Pavlov
3. Unconditioned stimulus, unconditioned response
4. conditioned stimulus, conditioned response
5. stimulus generalization
6. discrimination
7. extinction
8. John Watson
9. Little Albert
10. Mary Cover Jones; Peter
11. Operant conditioning
12. B. F. Skinner
13. primary reinforcer
14. secondary reinforcer
15. positive reinforcement
16. negative reinforcement
17. punishment
18. shaping
19. chaining
20. continuous reinforcement
21. schedules; partial reinforcement schedule
22. variable ratio schedule
23. fixed ratio schedule
24. fixed interval reinforcement
25. variable interval reinforcement
26. social learning;
27. observational learning
28. Albert Bandura
29. cognitive approach
30. knowledge
31. E. C. Tolman
32. cognitive maps
33. strategies.

Worksheet

WHO / WHAT AM I?

1. shaping
2. cognitive approach
3. Pavlov
4. cognitive map
5. conditioning
6. B. F. Skinner
7. extinction
8. social learning
9. Albert Bandura
10. punishment

POSITIVE AND NEGATIVE REINFORCEMENT OF BEHAVIORS

Situation I

a. Susie's
b. Jane's
c. staying up
d. stopping crying
e. crying
f. Jane allowing Susie to stay up

Situation II

a. Buffy's
b. Chris's
c. food
d. stopping begging
e, begging
f. giving food to the dog

Conditioning in Advertising - How Effective is it?

1. Doublemint chewing gum
2. Shower to Shower
3. Coke
4. AT&T telephone
5. Maxwell House Coffee
6. Jolly Green Giant
7. Wisk
8. Folger's
9. L'Oreal
10. Hallmark cards

Chapter 8

ANSWER KEY

Vocabulary Review

A. Answer to Crossword Puzzle

			¹O	V	E	²R	L	E	A	R	N	I	N	G			
						E											
						³C	H	U	N	K	I	N	G				
	⁴S	C	H	E	⁵M	A											
	H				⁶E	L	A	B	O	R	⁷A	T	I	O	N		
	O		⁸S			L					C						
	R		Y					⁹P		¹⁰L	O	N	G	T	E	R	¹¹M
	T		N					O		U							N
	T		A					S		S							E
	E		P			¹²E	I	D	E	T	I	C					M
	R		S					T		I							O
¹³A	M	N	E	S	I	A		I		¹⁴I	C	O	N	I	¹⁵C		N
								V		M					U		I
¹⁶I	N	¹⁷T	E	R	F	E	R	E	N	C	E				R		C
		R								M					V		D
		A				¹⁸S	E	N	S	O	R	Y			E		E
		N								R							V
		S			¹⁹M	E	M	O	²⁰R	Y							I
					E				O								C
			²¹I	N	F	O	R	M	A	T	I	O	N				E

Worksheet

1. schemas
2. attention
3. chunking
4. forgetting
5. mnemonic device
6. overlearning
7. recall
8. recognition
9. positive
10. iconic
11. amnesia
12. acoustic
13. short term
14. eidetic
15. negative

ANSWER KEY

Review/Test Preparation

1.	b	6.	a	11.	c	16.	d
2.	c	7.	c	12.	a	17.	a
3.	a	8.	b	13.	b	18.	b
4.	b	9.	d	14.	a	19.	d
5.	d	10.	c	15.	c	20.	d

True/False

1. True
2. True
3. False
4. True
5. True

Chapter 9

ANSWER KEY

Vocabulary

Word Search

```
T  I  N  T  L  L  E  R  B  L  S  C  H  I  O  T  L  E  S  C  A
C  O  N  E  A  E  V  E  R  B  A  L  S  C  A  L  E  S  C  A  N
I  N  T  T  L  L  I  G  V  E  R  B  S  C  D  A  L  E  C  N  O
E  L  A  B  E  R  A  T  I  O  N  V  E  R  A  L  I  N  T  E  I
L  A  T  V  E  L  S  C  A  L  V  R  B  L  P  S  C  L  I  N  T
A  C  O  U  T  I  L  E  N  D  I  R  E  C  T  I  O  N  V  B  E
C  O  M  P  R  H  S  I  N  C  P  R  E  T  A  T  I  O  N  S  L
S  Y  S  T  H  O  U  M  G  R  I  S  C  A  B  A  L  C  O  M  P
E  S  M  B  R  E  A  K  S  E  T  B  R  K  I  E  A  K  S  E  M
C  S  E  T  R  A  K  E  S  S  N  E  T  V  L  I  T  Y  B  L  O
N  I  N  T  E  L  L  I  G  E  N  C  E  T  I  G  E  N  C  E  C
A  T  T  E  N  G  E  N  I  N  C  R  E  A  T  I  V  I  T  Y  E
M  E  A  G  E  N  C  E  C  R  E  A  T  Q  Y  I  E  R  B  A  R
R  M  L  A  N  C  E  P  E  R  F  S  C  A  U  L  E  G  E  N  U
O  L  A  A  C  S  E  C  N  A  C  S  F  R  E  O  P  E  R  U  C
F  O  G  N  O  I  T  A  D  R  A  T  E  R  L  A  T  N  E  M  C
R  M  E  N  T  R  E  T  A  R  T  I  O  N  M  E  N  I  A  T  I
E  M  O  C  C  O  M  P  R  E  H  E  N  S  I  O  N  S  E  T  P
P  R  E  H  E  N  T  E  S  S  A  O  B  J  A  S  E  M  B  N  Y
P  E  R  F  O  Y  L  B  M  E  S  S  A  T  C  E  J  B  O  N  T
```

A.

1. h	6. l	11. b
2. m	7. a	12. e
3. f	8. c	13. i
4. m	9. d	14. k
5. g	10. j	

B. 1. Stanford Binet: 2. self-evaluation:

   3. Individual intelligence tests: 4. Group intelligence tests:

Review/Test

1. intelligence
2. Minister of France asked Binet to develop a test to locate students not bright enough to be in regular school system; Alfred Binet
3. a. direction   b. adaptability   c. comprehension   d. self-evaluation
4. 140, 80, 120
5. verbal, performance scale
6. influence of society
7. identical twins
8. Individual intelligence tests, group intelligence tests
9. white middle class group
10. creative

Chapter 9

ANSWER KEY

11. set, breaking set
12. Mental retardation
    a. IQ 70-79, slow learners, fail to complete high school
    b. IQ 52-67, most attend special schools
    c. IQ 36-51, physical problems, trainable, but need supervision
    d. IQ 20-35, require constant supervision
    e. IQ 19 or below. Smallest group, rarely mature beyond two years mentally, constant care required
13. see text
14. theory of multiple intelligences.

Worksheet

1. group intelligence test
2. mental retardation
3. multiple intelligences theory
4. direction, adaptability, comprehension, self-evaluation
5. borderline, mild, moderate, severe, profound
6. set, breaking set
7. intelligence
8. Alfred Binet
9. Stanford Binet
10. intelligence quotient

1. Intelligence is the ability to understand and adapt to the environment by using a combination inherited abilities and learning experiences. Creativity is mental processes that result in origin workable ideas
2. verbal scale is based on word usage; performance scale is based on performing certain tasks

Chapter 10

ANSWER KEY

Vocabulary Review

Use definitions at the end of the chapter and those included within the context of the chapter.

Worksheet

1. nature/nurture
2. maturation
3. feral
4. nuclear family
5. self-esteem
6. critical period
7. extended family
8. imprinting
9. heredity
10. separation

Review/Test Preparation

A.
1. b
2. d
3. c
4. d
5. a

B.
1. True
2. True
3. False
4. False
5. False
6. True
7. True
8. False
9. True
10. False

C.
1. maturation
2. critical period
3. feral
4. physical, psychological
5. separation anxiety
6. sensorimotor stage; preoperational stage, concrete operations, formal operations
7. principle of reversibility
8. Conservation
9. other children, brothers and sisters, school, teachers, the general environment
10. environment

Chapter 11

ANSWER KEY

Vocabulary

1. a	6. s	11. g	16. q	21. l	26. f	31.
2. h	7. x	12. b	17. dd	22. o	27. k
3. e	8. z	13. m	18. aa	23. y	28. u
4. n	9. bb	14. t	19. c	24. cc	29. d
5. p	10. ee	15. w	20. j	25. r	30. i

Review/Test Preparation

a.   Multiple choice

1. b	6. b
2. a	7. b
3. c	8. c
4. c	9. d
5. d	10. c

b.   Fill in blanks

1. early adolescence, middle adolescence, late adolescence
2. puberty
3. pituitary gland, adrenal glands, gonads
4. growth spurts
5. anorexia nervosa
6. rite of passage
7. cliques
8. gangs
9. group identity versus alienation
10. identity, identity confusion
11. fidelity
12. negative identity
13. identity achievement
14. Formal Operations
15. social contracts stage, universal ethical principles stage

ANSWER KEY

Word Scramble

```
D  L  A  T  E  A  D  O  L  E  S  C  E  N  C  E  N
N  A  T  E  A  D  M  U  I  R  O  T  A  R  O  M  Y
A  R  F  O  R  E  C  L  O  S  U  R  E  S  U  R  E
L  F  O  R  E  I  D  E  L  U  R  U  S  U  R  E  L
G  A  N  F  I  D  E  L  T  R  E  P  G  A  N  D  S
Y  D  R  I  T  E  O  F  P  A  S  S  A  G  E  R  N
R  I  T  D  U  N  A  L  A  S  A  H  P  O  A  R  D
A  P  U  E  B  T  O  T  Y  I  D  T  A  N  E  N  Y
T  U  I  L  T  I  A  I  R  Y  G  W  E  A  M  C  G
I  T  O  I  N  T  E  N  S  E  N  O  H  D  E  N  T
U  I  T  T  Y  Y  A  R  Y  U  A  R  L  S  I  O  N
T  T  Y  Y  G  L  D  E  N  T  F  G  T  Y  C  R  I
I  D  E  N  T  I  T  Y  C  O  N  F  U  S  I  O  N
P  U  B  E  R  T  Y  I  D  E  N  C  I  N  F  U  S
F  I  D  E  H  O  R  M  O  N  E  S  L  D  I  T  Y
```

1.	late adolescence	8.	gang
2.	puberty	9.	identity
3.	hormones	10.	identity confusion
4.	gonads	11.	moratorium
5.	pituitary gland	12.	fidelity
6.	growth spurt	13.	diffusion
7.	rite of passage	14.	foreclosure

ANSWER KEY

Crossword Puzzle

¹A	R	²T	E	R	I	O	³S	C	L	E	R	O	S	I	S
L		H					E								⁴H
Z		A		⁵M	E	N	O	P	A	U	S	E			O
H		N		I		I									S
E		A		⁶D		L									P
I		T		L		E		⁶E							I
M		O		I				M							C
E		L		F				P							E
R		O		⁷G	E	R	O	N	T	O	L	O	G	Y	
S		G						Y							
		Y													

Review/Test Preparation

1. late adolescence/early adulthood, mid-life transition, middle adulthood, late adulthood
2. marriage, career, children
3. reflection, reevaluation
4. withdrawn, detached, sense of humor, playfulness, career, companionship
5. anxiety, guilt, conflicts
6. midlife crisis
7. marital satisfaction
8. "feminine" "masculine"
9. empty nest period
10. menopause
11. late adulthood
12. gerontology
13. cellular time clocks
14. senility
15. cerebral arteriosclerosis
16. Alzheiver's Disease
17. poor health, social isolation, no social meaningfulness
18. isolation, bereavement
19. Thanatology
20. (1) loss of mastery over oneself
    (2) separation from loved ones
    (3) gnawing fear of being replaced by another
21. denial, anger, bargaining depression, acceptance
22. Hospices

Chapter 13

ANSWER KEY

Vocabulary

1. identification
2. androgen
3. premenstrual syndrome
4. gender
5. gender role behavior
6. androgyny
7. hormone
8. menstrual cycle
9. estrogen
10. spatial skills

Review/Test Preparation

1. c
2. b
3. d
4. b
5. a
6. a
7. d
8. c
9. a
10. d
11. a
12. a
13. c
14. d
15. b
16. b
17. c
18. a
19. b
20. b

Worksheet

1. hormones
2. androgen, estrogen
3. involved in reproduction
4. activity level
5. Spatial skill
6. environmental influences
7. no notable difference exists
8. just as achievement-oriented as males
9. menstrual cycles
10. Premenstrual syndrome
11. Gender role behavior
12. androgyny

Chapter14

ANSWER KEY

Vocabulary

1. Y	6. E	11. FF	16. DD	21. Q	26. EE	31. AA
2. S	7. X	12. K	17. I	22. F	27. B	32. R
3. H	8. Z	13. A	18. L	23. BB	28. N	33. G
4. II	9. M	14. O	19. W	24. U	29. GG	34. V
5. D	10. T	15. C	20. HH	25. J	30. CC	35. P

Review/Test Preparation

1. psychoanalysis
2. Sigmund Freud
3. hysteria
4. unconscious
5. free association
6. repression
7. libido
8. id, superego, ego
9. oral stage
10. anal stage
11. phallic stage
12. latency stage
13. genital stage
14. Carl Jung
15. persona
16. neoFreudians
17. Karen Horney
18. Adler
19. Erik Erikson
20. behaviorism
21. B. F. Skinner
22. Reinforcements
23. modeling
24. humanistic
25. ideal self
26. fully functioning individu
27. self-actualized
28. personality traits

29. (a) how well people get along in social situations, (b) how traditional the person is, (c) h comfortable one feels

30. (a) degree of friendliness, (b) how eager they are to do different or novel things, (c) how anxi or comfortable they feel.

Worksheet

1. Freud
2. Skinner
3. Jung
4. Horney
5. Adler
6. Erikson
7. Bandura
8. Rogers
9. Maslow

Chapter15

ANSWER KEY

Vocabulary

1. reverse halo
2. California Psychological Inventory
3. projective test
4. situational assessment
5. Barnum effect
6. norms
7. reliability
8. psychological test
9. aptitude test
10. Strong-Campbell Interest test
11. achievement test
12. personality inventory
13. validity
14. halo effect
15. standoutishness
16. Rorschach test
17. aptitude
18. vocational interest test

Review/Test Preparation

1. d
2. b
3. c
4. b
5. a
6. c
7. b
8. c
9. a
10. c
11. d
12. a
13. b
14. c
15. a
16. a

Worksheet

1. Scholastic Aptitude Test
2. reverse halo
3. halo effect
4. standoutishness
5. establishing norms
6. valid
7. reliable
8. personality test
9. projective tests
10. Rorschach Ink Blot Test
11. aptitude
12. Achievement tests
13. vocational interest tests
14. Strong-Campbell Interest Inventory
15. situational assessment

Chapter16

ANSWER KEY

Vocabulary Review

1.	s	11.	x	21.	h	31.	t
2.	b	12.	bb	22.	p	32.	f
3.	w	13.	ff	23.	u	33.	j
4.	1	14.	a	24.	aa		
5.	g	15.	r	25.	ee		
6.	dd	16.	m	26.	v		
7.	0	17.	y	27.	d		
8.	e	18.	cc	28.	k		
9.	n	19.	gg	29.	q		
10.	i	20.	c	30.	z		

Worksheet

A. crust, fresh, raven, intone; frustration

B. flick, ocean, circle, stone; conflicts

C. office, tight   valor, knight; fight or flight

D. elate. poodle, psyche, logic; psychological

E. reach, street, shave, pause; stress

F. nerd, pansy, grist, icing; synergistic

Test Review

1.	a	6.	c
2.	b	7.	a
3.	b	8.	c
4.	d	9.	a
5.	c	10.	b

Chapter17

ANSWER KEY

Vocabulary Review

1. distraction
2. endorphin
3. antibodies
4. defense mechanism
5. cognitive
6. muscle contraction headache
7. repression
8. sudden death phenomenon
9. projection
10. immune system
11. migraine
12. ulcer
13. asthma
14. denial
15. regression
16. placebo effect
17. phantom limb pain
18. acupuncture
19. cognitive strategy
20. rationalization
21. biofeedback
22. redefinition

Review/Test Preparation

1. true
2. true
3. false
4. true
5. true
6. false
7. false
8. true
9. false
10. false
11. true
12. true
13. true
14. false
15. true
16. true
17. false
18. true
19. false
20. true
21. false
22. true
23. true
24. true
25. false

Worksheet

1. rationalization
2. repression
3. projection
4. regression
5. denial

Chapter18

ANSWER KEY

Vocabulary

1.	T	11.	M	21.	D	31.	F
2.	G	12.	Y	22.	K	32.	FF
3.	P	13.	U	23.	X		
4.	L	14.	R	24.	O		
5.	V	15.	BB	25.	J		
6.	Z	16.	N	26.	EE		
7.	A	17.	H	27.	C		
8.	I	18.	Q	28.	S		
9.	CC	19.	AA	29.	E		
10.	B	20.	DD	30.	W		

Review/Test Preparation

1.	False	6.	False	11.	True	16.	True
2.	True	7.	True	12.	True		
3.	True	8.	True	13.	False		
4.	False	9.	False	14.	True		
5.	True	10.	True	15.	False		

17. a. through disorder   b. hallucinations
    c. delusions   d. inappropriate emotional responses

18. a. major depression   b. slow speech
    c. severe loss of appetite   d. sense of hopelessness
    e. extreme feelings of worthlessness   f. thoughts of death and suicide

19. a. agitation   b. restlessness
    c. inability to concentrate   d. extremely rapid speech-flight 0f ideas

20. wild swings of mood from up to down

21. hallucinations and delusions

22. psychotic episodes

23. dopamina

24. psychopaths

25. a lack of conscience

Chapter 19

ANSWER KEY

Vocabulary

1.	F	11.	CC	21.	M
2.	I	12.	AA	22.	E
3.	R	13.	A	23.	P
4.	W	14.	U	24.	D
5.	N	15.	Q	25.	K
6.	C	16.	BB	26.	G
7.	0	17.	B	27.	L
8.	H	18.	Z	28.	X
9.	S	19.	T	29.	V
10.	Y	20.	J		

Review/Test Preparation

1. Philippe Pinel
2. psychologist - Ph.D. Work directly with people in clinical situation: psychiatrist - M. D. specialize in the mental health field.
3. psychiatric social worker.
4. psychiatric nurse
5. psychotherapies
6. psychotherapists
7. psychoanalysis
8. free association
9. transference
10. humanistic
11. client-centered therapy
12. Carl Rogers
13. nondirective therapy
14. unconditional positive regard
15. behavioral therapy
16. systematic desensitization
17. aversive conditioning
18. Albert Ellis
19. Rational Emotive Therapy
20. encounter group
21. chemotherapy
22. electroconvulsive therapy
23. psychosurgery
24. group therapy
25. internalized sentences

Chapter 20

ANSWER KEY

Crossword puzzle.

r1	[1]A	T	T	R	I	B	U	T	I	O	N	T	H	E	O	[2]R	Y
r2	N															I	
r3	[3]A	T	T	R	I	B	U	T	I	O	N				[4]P	S	
r4	E														E	K	
r5	[5]C	O	N	S	E	Q	U	E	N	C	E	S			R	Y	
r6	E														S	S	
r7	D														O	H	
r8	[6]D	E	I	N	D	[7]I	V	I	D	U	A	T	I	O	N	I	
r9	N					M									A	[8]F	[9]E
r10	T					I			[10]C						L	[11]T	V
r11	S			[12]C	A	T	H	A	R	S	I	S			S		A
r12						A			O						P		L
r13	[13]D	E	N	S	I	T	Y		W						A		U
r14						I			D						C		A
r15						O			I						E		T
r16						N			N								I
r17									G								O
r18																	N
r19		[14]T	E	R	R	I	T	O	R	I	A	L	I	T	Y		

Review/Test Preparation

1.	c	6.	b	11.	b
2.	b	7.	b	12.	d
3.	a	8.	b	13.	c
4.	b	9.	c	14.	a
5.	d	10.	d	15.	d

Chapter 21

ANSWER KEY

Vocabulary - see answers in chapter content.

Review/Test Preparation

1. internalize
2. reference group
3. stereotyping
4. prejudice
5. illusory correlation
6. face-to-face, remote
7. scapegoat
8. joining new reference groups, to put ourselves in the place of others
9. cognitive dissonance
10. Stanley Milgram
11. immunizer, verbal persuasion
12. polygraph
13. does not
14. friendliness, sensory deprivation, reward system
15. compliance with a small request, reward, larger request

Worksheet

1. deter, zeal, lining; internalize
2. prose, story, steep; stereotype
3. taper, goal, cross; scapegoat
4. judge, write, price; prejudice
5. freedom, current, purge; reference group
6. grope, happy, loyal; polygraph